A Girl Aboard the
TITANIC

A Girl Aboard the

TITANIC

A Survivor's Story

EVA HART

AS TOLD TO RON DENNEY

AMBERLEY

This edition first published 2012

Amberley Publishing
The Hill, Stroud
Gloucestershire, GL5 4EP

www.amberley-books.com

British Library Cataloguing in Publication Data.
A catalogue record for this book is available from the British Library.

ISBN 978 1 4456 0089 5

Typeset in 12pt on 13.5pt Celeste OT.
Typesetting and Origination by Amberley Publishing.
Printed in the UK.

CONTENTS

PREFACE

The subject of this biography was a little girl of seven years when she was taken by her parents on the *Titanic*'s maiden voyage to emigrate to Canada. Her mother had a strong premonition that the trip would end in disaster – as it did, causing the death of Eva Hart's father.

This biography tells the story of the little girl before emigrating, her vivid memory of the tragedy that cost more than 1,500 lives, and the difficulties faced by her and her mother as they struggled to rebuild their lives back in England. It covers the problems they encountered in making a fresh life for themselves and Miss Hart's initial attempts to push aside, and then eventually to live with her memories.

Throughout the story the shadow of the *Titanic* can be felt upon the life of first the little girl, then the young woman and finally the mature woman. A shadow which lifts as she freely talks on radio and television about the terrible journey that so changed her destiny and future. It shows the way in which it dominated her thoughts in her old age as scientists sought to find the wreck of what was once the world's most luxurious liner, and the grave of Eva Hart's father.

The effects of the *Titanic* are reflected in actions and public service throughout her life until her death. Many books have been written about the *Titanic* and the tragic loss of life that occurred when she struck an iceberg on the night of Sunday 14 April 1912 on her maiden voyage from Southampton to New York.

The ship and its short existence also has a major role to play in the book, but it is only a supporting role. One side of the *Titanic* disaster that has never been adequately covered has been the aftermath on the people affected by the tragedy and at this late stage that can probably never be fully treated. But in this particular instance we are able to follow the story of someone who, as a young girl, survived the disaster which killed her father. We can then see how that affected and influenced her whole life. Inevitably, it can only be one of the many lives that were touched by the tragedy, but in numerous ways it is representative of the trials, tribulations and sufferings of those who lived after seeing so many die.

Eva Hart was one of the longest living survivors, for eighty-four years after the event. She tells her story from her early childhood memories before leaving England to the disaster itself, through her years of growing up and to her later years involving talks and interviews about her life and the tragedy that did so much to shape it.

Throughout it all the *Titanic* casts its spell, showing that it cannot be forgotten or ignored even after all these years. Miss Hart does not seek to allay that spell, but to show in her own way that if one is given a life to live it should be lived to the full, without regret, with fortitude, good humour and a sense of public responsibility.

This is the story of a remarkable and exceptional woman.

Ronald C. Denney

I

PRELUDE TO A NIGHTMARE

The world's largest, most expensive and most glamorous ship was dying. After only five days of her maiden voyage she had been mortally damaged by an iceberg. Her death had been slow and drawn out for more than two and a half hours as the icy waters of the Atlantic Ocean gradually filled first her holds, and then her decks one by one. Eventually she sank, taking with her more than fifteen hundred people – passengers, officers and crew. All the time, we, the few survivors in the totally inadequate lifeboats, looked on – hearing the screams and cries for help from those drowning and rapidly freezing to death.

Everybody felt numb, not just from the cold, but more from the traumatic experience we had all just undergone. Only a short time before we had all been passengers or crew on the world's newest and most luxurious ocean liner. Now only a few hundred of us remained, expecting some fresh disaster to engulf us as we sobbed over the loss of relations, friends and possessions. Our small lifeboats floated aimlessly with nowhere to go, bobbing about like ducks on a lake; but this was no lake and the whole thing was horrifyingly real. Few of the survivors fully realised how bad the situation was at the time and those of us who were children were mainly concerned with the cold, the wet and the general discomfort, and in some cases with trying to find our parents from whom we had become separated.

We were over 600 miles from the nearest port, surrounded by icebergs, in freezing temperatures, with no food and very few lights. We did not know whether or not any other ship had picked up the distress calls from the stricken liner before she had sunk. If they had heard the signals, would they have taken them seriously or have dismissed them as some form of prank [This was the initial reaction by the Officer of the Watch on the *Virginian* when he heard the news; see G Marcus, *The Maiden Voyage,* p. 169]; after all, the *Titanic* was supposed to be unsinkable.

Witnessing the sinking of any ship is a frightful experience and more so when a short time before you have been a passenger on that very ship. One moment you are part of an active, thriving community, then all that changes and a little while later you are watching and hearing the death throes as it slowly slides below the waves, until it eventually disappears from sight leaving a great visual void and an emptiness inside you.

I have lived and re-lived the dying moments of the *Titanic* many times since I sat cold and miserable, crying for my father in that small lifeboat bobbing about on the icy waters of the Atlantic over eighty years ago. Being only seven years old when it happened I certainly did not realise how the *Titanic* disaster was going to affect my whole life, but I knew that I was witnessing something quite horrifying that I would never be able to forget. Somehow, even at that stage, I was conscious of the fact that I was never going to see my father again.

During my lifetime it has been impossible to escape from the story of the *Titanic* or to ignore my own involvement in the tragedy. In my early years I did my best to shut it out of my mind, but its impact was regularly renewed with press stories, books and films all presenting different aspects of what occurred, often contentious and sometimes highly inaccurate. As I am now one of the few remaining survivors of the disaster I have, during the past forty years, played a small part in trying to prevent distortions of the events, as I know them, from arising or being perpetuated. For this reason I have frequently told my story at meetings, on radio and television and for press articles. For me this has served as a mental release from the memories of that voyage and that night of tragedy which so changed my life.

Our presence on that ill-fated ship in April 1912 was almost by accident and had no origin in any desire just to travel on a ship because it was on its maiden voyage. We were, in fact, emigrating to Canada where my father was expecting to set up in the construction business with a friend. But, of course, my story really starts a few years before then.

I was born in the London suburb of Seven Kings, an area which now forms part of the London Borough of Redbridge. Both of my parents were quite old for starting a family when I was born as their first and only child. My mother, Esther, had first been married when she was eighteen years old. She had led a very unhappy married life and was eventually widowed in her early thirties. During the intervening years she had borne nine children, none of whom survived for more than a few months. This was due to a combination of the physical assaults she suffered at the hands of her first husband during her pregnancies and the rare blood group she possessed and which I have inherited. Because of the misery she had endured she had said she would never marry again and returned to live with her parents.

It was several years later that her father sought the services of a local builder in order to have a new house constructed in the nearby village of Chadwell Heath. The man who called to discuss the job was Benjamin Hart, who up to that time had remained single while building up his construction business. Apparently, he went home after talking over the contract and announced to his father 'I've met the woman I'm going to marry'.

So, despite her original intentions, my mother married in 1900 for the second time, when she was thirty-seven and her new husband was thirty-six. I was born four-and-a-half years later in January 1905 when both my parents were middle-aged. So I became the tenth child my mother had carried, but the only one to survive. To my parents I was something very special. At the time of the *Titanic* disaster my mother was forty-nine and my father forty-eight, and by then I was seven years old.

My parents were quite different in their looks. Mother was above average height for a woman, solidly build, with a fairly full face. She had very fair hair and the most beautiful green-grey eyes. Father was a little shorter than mother and was sturdily built because of the nature of his work. His outstanding feature was his lovely black wavy hair that I used to like to run my hands through when he was sitting in the armchair reading his newspaper. When I was young I looked very much like my father, but as I have grown older have acquired much more of my mother's looks with a fuller face.

We lived in New Road, Seven Kings and my father had become a well-known master builder in that area. Seven Kings adjoins the town of Ilford, now an eastern suburb of London, and was at that time a developing area on the edge of the Essex countryside. Beyond Seven Kings to the east was the expanding area of Goodmayes and the small villages of Chadwell Heath and Dagenham which were to grow enormously when engulfed later by the big London expansion which occurred after the First World War.

Even by modern standards we were comfortably placed. My mother had people to help in the house and my father owned a motor car at a time when they were still luxuries which only enthusiasts and business men could afford. The first car I can recall my father owning was an Argyll which possessed the, now unusual, feature of having a passenger door at the rear. Because it was quite a small car he later sold it in order to obtain one which was larger and more comfortable. We had this second car until he sold everything prior to our emigration on the *Titanic*.

From an early age I was accustomed to being driven in a pony and trap by my mother along country lanes and over uneven roads. But I greatly enjoyed travelling by car and on one occasion we went, on what in those days was a long car journey, to visit my mother's relations at Rye in Sussex. We also used to drive into the surrounding Essex countryside to visit various friends. The big outward growth of London had not started at that time, so that Hainault, Harold Hill, Loughton and Debden were still rural areas within easy reach of our home. We greatly enjoyed our trips out together and my mother made no secret of the fact that her whole life had changed for the better with her second marriage.

As most of my father's work was in the local area I was fortunate in being able to see a great deal of him. Although he was a busy man he always seemed to find time to play with me. I used to enjoy watching him work, taking great care over some particular part of a house, such as shaping a window frame or cutting joints. It was great fun playing amongst the wood shavings in his carpentry workroom, and the smell of freshly planed wood even now rekindles the pleasant memories of that happy time many years ago.

Because of my mother's previous unhappy marriage and the fact that I was her only surviving child, we were a very close family. My mother loved my father dearly and I adored both my parents. I can only recall being smacked once by my father in the few years I knew him. It was so exceptional that it still sticks in my mind. It was a morning when my father was taking me to feed the ducks in South Park, Seven Kings. As we walked down the garden path he saw a friend who greeted him with, 'Do you know the King is dead?' My father immediately said, 'I must go in and put on a black tie.' At that I started kicking up a fuss, saying it was more important to feed the ducks than to put on a black tie, not appreciating the significance of the King's death. My father was so angry that without more ado he smacked me. I never did see the ducks that day, but the sudden death of King Edward VII on 6 May 1910, when I was only five years old, was firmly imprinted on my mind and elsewhere.

Our life in Seven Kings appeared to me to be a very happy one. However, during 1911 business was not too good and, incredible as it may seem in these days of persistent house shortages, my father had many long suburban roads of houses all marked 'To Let' and no customers for them. That meant substantial sums of money and capital were tied up and this became a major worry to him. I imagine he had come to a point in his life when he was taking a hard look into the future and could see only a continued period of uncertainty ahead.

About this time we had a visit from a friend of his who had gone to Canada some years before and had come back for a vacation. He told us what a marvellous country Canada was and how well he was doing with the expansion taking place in the various Canadian cities and towns. In the space of that one evening, which I think lasted well into the early hours of the next morning, father had made up his mind to cut his losses in England and to emigrate to Canada in order to set up in business with his friend. They were going to build part of what is now the city of Winnipeg. It was still quite small in 1912, of course, and if my father's plans had worked out it would have changed the whole pattern of my life. At the end of the vacation his friend returned to Canada on a different ship which arrived quite safely, and within a very few years he was extremely wealthy. As it was, my father died when the *Titanic* sank, at a time when his finances were apparently at their lowest ebb. Although I was not fully aware of the situation at that time I did know that there were difficulties which he hoped to overcome by re-starting in Canada. Once he had taken the decision after that long night's discussion he became very keen about going and was excited at the prospect of life for us in Canada.

As soon as possible he booked a cabin for us in a small ship called the *Philadelphia*. It was all settled very quickly and the only person who was terribly unhappy about the whole thing was my mother. From the very beginning she became apprehensive. She was frightened by the whole idea. It was totally unlike her normal, sensible, level-headed self and she didn't know the reason for it. I remember my father saying to her testily many times, 'I don't know what you are frightened of. I don't know why you are getting in such a state about it. What is it you are frightened of?'

And she used to say, 'I don't know. I don't know what it is, but every time I think about it I am certain that this is the wrong thing to do.'

Despite her feelings, no one would listen to her. Even her own parents said, 'You are going to miss a wonderful opportunity if you don't go. We can't understand why you are so hesitant and unhappy about it.'

My mother's apprehension did nothing to deter my father from taking the necessary steps for the emigration. He decided that we should travel to Canada via New York in order to visit his sister who was living there and whom he had not seen for many years. The intention was that we would then continue our journey to Canada by train. He had thought it would be better than any other route as the St Lawrence river was going to be frozen at that time of year and that would have meant disembarking at Halifax and travelling across Canada by train in any case.

We were in the process of selling the house and getting rid of the furniture and then, when all the final arrangements were in hand our plans were completely thrown upside down. The combination of a coal strike and a dock strike, both of these very serious, meant that the *Philadelphia* would not be sailing on its pre-arranged date. I think my mother was very pleased when this news arrived and she felt it was a good reason not to go to Canada at all. But my father was rather upset about the delay and started to worry the shipping company responsible for arranging our journey. He constantly pestered their offices and pointed out that he was not indulging in a pleasure trip but that the whole of our future life depended upon his reaching Canada by a particular date.

Because he was so bothered about the *Philadelphia* not sailing, the shipping company tried to find an alternative ship that was due to sail at about the same time. He thought it was marvellous news when he was told that we could have second class accommodation on the *Titanic,* which was being prepared for its maiden voyage early in April.

Everybody had heard about this fabulous new liner being constructed for the White Star Line and my father told us all about the comfort we could expect and what a good ship it was. He certainly could not afford the cost of the first class accommodation in the *Titanic,* as in some instances that was more than £900, at 1912 prices! But he was prepared to pay the difference between the fare he had already paid for the *Philadelphia* and the larger amount needed for the second class on the new liner, knowing that the four-berth cabin allocated would be quite comfortable and adequate for the three of us. It was when we learnt of the possibility of travelling on the *Titanic* that a light dawned on my mother and she said, 'I haven't known up 'till now why I do not want to go. But now I do know.'

'Well, that's something,' my father said. 'You say you know now. That's fine, why don't you want to go?'

I remember her answer as clearly as if I could hear her speaking the words now. 'Because this is the ship that they say is unsinkable,' she replied, 'and that is flying in the face of the Almighty. That ship will never reach the other side.'

Even at this stage nobody would listen to her and everybody thought she was being very foolish, particularly as the *Titanic* was the most modern and best equipped ship in the world. A number of people did point out how this premonition of the ship sinking was so utterly out of character and unlike her. She was not a superstitious woman, nor given to flights of fancy as perhaps a younger woman might have been. She was middle-aged and her earlier experiences meant she was normally very down-to-earth and level-headed. She had had a great deal of happiness in the relatively few years since she had remarried and the thought of losing this upset her greatly. She had a premonition that something dreadful was going to happen, but didn't know what. She got into quite a state about it as she was absolutely certain this would be the end of her happiness; and nothing would convince her otherwise.

But eventually we went. Along with many other passengers, we joined the White Star Line boat train at Waterloo Station at 9.45 a.m. on Wednesday 10 April 1912.

2

THE UNSINKABLE *TITANIC*

Waterloo Railway Station was alive with the hustle and bustle of porters carrying luggage, people saying goodbye, whistles blowing and flags waving. To avoid an early morning rush we had stayed overnight with my mother's brother, Uncle Harry, at his London flat. He had decided to come and see us off on our journey. As we waited for the boat train to start I thought what a marvellous adventure it was and wondered what Canada would be like. I was totally unaware that we were in the company of some of the wealthiest people in the world, such as John Jacob Astor and Benjamin Guggenheim, most of them returning to the USA after spending the autumn and winter in Europe. All that concerned me was that we were on our way to Southampton where the *Titanic* was berthed and within a few days we would all be starting a new life in a foreign country.

The train journey was uneventful and the steam engine pulled the carriages into Southampton docks alongside the marvellous ship which towered out of the water above us like a large block of apartments. The *Titanic* had been constructed alongside her sister ship, the *Olympic,* at the Harland and Wolff shipyards in Belfast. At that time she was the largest ship ever built and was also considered to be the most luxurious liner in the world. Nothing comparable has ever been built to the same standards of opulence and comfort, designed to attract the wealthy trend-setters from the leading US families. Even the third class (steerage) facilities were considered to be exceptional at that time, with good ventilation, heating and electric lighting. The fare for the poor immigrants traveling in that part of the ship was about £13 (at 1912 prices).

Although radio was still in its infancy, the *Titanic* was fitted with the most up-to-date equipment operated by the Marconi Marine Company and surpassed only by that fitted to her sister ship, the *Olympic*. The range of the radio was up to 400 miles during the day and extended to 2,000 miles at night-time. The Marconi Company provided two officers to work on the *Titanic* in order to have a twenty-four hour service. This enabled many passengers to send messages to their friends and relations who were expecting them to arrive in New York on Monday, 15th, or Tuesday, 16 April, 1912.

The *Titanic* had been termed 'unsinkable' because the whole length of the hull consisted of a double bottom divided up into a cellular structure for additional strength. Above this the hull was separated into sixteen watertight compartments by bulkheads built transversely across the ship. Unfortunately, the impression given by the design of the ship was misleading, as, in fact, she was only unsinkable if no more than four of the watertight compartments were breached in a collision – as we were eventually to find out to our cost.

However, the ship more than satisfied the British Board of Trade requirements that existed in 1912. As part of her equipment she was required to carry sixteen lifeboats with a minimum total capacity of 5,500 cubic feet, plus additional rafts and floats equivalent to 75 per cent of the lifeboat capacity. In addition to the required number of lifeboats the liner also carried four collapsible lifeboats (called Engelhardts). These gave a total lifeboat capacity of fewer than a thousand people. Nobody seemed greatly worried that these were only sufficient to cater for about half the people on the ship in the event of an emergency taking place during the maiden voyage. I very much doubt if any passengers embarking on the ship, other than my mother, gave any real thought to the possibility of the ship sinking in any case. It is, however, only fair to say that the Board of Trade regulations for ocean-going liners had been questioned at an earlier date by Horatio Bottomley MP, in the House of Commons but this had not resulted in any action being taken. The inadequacy of the regulations concerning lifeboats and safety at sea in general had really arisen because of the rapid growth in size of passenger liners, which was greater than had been anticipated when the regulations had been drawn up.

The crew on the ship had been specially selected from the other ships in the White Star fleet and included many well qualified and highly skilled ships' officers. The Captain, Edward J. Smith, had spent thirty-two years in the service of the White Star Line alone and was due to retire after taking the *Titanic* through its maiden voyage. He was one of the many who died when the ship sank.

Like the rest of the ship, the cabins were exceptionally comfortable. Photographs taken at the time show the first class cabins with brass bedsteads, marble washstands, armchairs and sofas and with fans in the ceilings. Many companies considered it a great honour to have provided items for the ship and this was proudly declared in their advertisements. For instance, one manufacturer was able to boast that 'By the provision of Vinolia Otto Toilet Soap for her first-class passengers the *Titanic* also leads as offering a higher standard of Toilet Luxury and comfort at sea'.

I cannot remember which brand of soap we had in the second class, but our cabin on the port side of the ship was also very nice. As it was a four berth cabin, we only had three of the tiered bunks lowered and this made it much easier for moving around. We had ample cupboards for all our clothes and the cabin had its own wash-hand basin and a dressing table as well as a couple of comfortable chairs. My bunk was beneath the one used by my father, and much of the time it was occupied by my doll and teddy bear which I had taken to keep me company.

Even as we climbed the gangplank to board the ship my mother had continued to try and persuade father not to proceed with the voyage. But once we were on board and had found our cabin and settled down, she accepted the situation. In a very firm voice she said to him, 'Now let us have no more arguments, no more unhappiness, no more trouble about this. I have come, we are here, the ship has sailed. But now I am going to be quite determined, and no matter what you may say I will never go to bed in this ship at night. I shall sit up all night and shall go to bed in the daytime.'

This was a most unusual way for her to speak and it undoubtedly took father by surprise. 'Of course, if you want to be stupid I can't prevent you' he said to her, 'but I don't know what you think other people will say.' 'I don't mind what they say' she replied, 'but I shall not go to bed at night on this ship.' She was quite determined on her line of action and stuck to it. During the voyage she kept saying that she felt as if a large, black eagle was sitting on her shoulder and she was unable to shake it off. Whatever it was, I know that it was only due to her determination and obduracy that I lived to tell the tale. Had she been asleep at the time of the disaster we would not have been on deck in time to get into a lifeboat.

The *Titanic* sailed from Southampton at 12 noon that Wednesday, initially to go to Cherbourg to embark more passengers later that day, and then with a second stop at Queenstown (Cobh Harbour) in Ireland at 10.30 a.m. on Thursday 11 April. The majority of passengers embarking at the second stop were Irish emigrants travelling steerage to the 'New World'. On leaving Queenstown at 2.00 p.m. the ship was carrying 1,316 passengers and 891 crew. This is the best available figure. There has always been some conflict over the true number of passengers and crew carried, just as there has over the number of survivors. The Board of Trade in Great Britain published figures of 1,308 passengers and 898 crew, but these are said to include one crew member who deserted the ship at Queenstown and several White Star Line employees travelling as passengers.

During the days which followed from midday on the Wednesday to midnight on the Saturday, the pattern of our lives was that mother slept all day, during which time my father looked after me. I had most of my meals with him and then when the time came for me to get ready for bed my mother would get up. She would then bath me, put me to bed and then dress herself before going up to dinner. She would spend the evening with my father and the other passengers, then when everyone else went to bed she used to sit fully dressed with her sewing or her reading. And she did this for each of the five nights we were at sea in the *Titanic.*

Other people in the second class learnt all about this and became accustomed to seeing her only at the two meals of breakfast and dinner each day. She never appeared for lunch. When they saw her at breakfast they would sometimes laugh and twit her and say 'What have you heard during the night?' and, 'Are you taking care of us?' They certainly did not take her foreboding seriously and obviously thought she was worrying about nothing.

During these few days I had a marvellous time being looked after by my father, who adored me. He was much less strict with me than my mother and I, in my turn, adored him and was delighted to have so much of his time. He played with me, took me to the nursery, bought me toys and together we explored as much of the ship as we possibly could. I greatly enjoyed those days when I had my father so much to myself.

In the course of our explorations I made friends with a little dog and spent a great deal of time playing with it. I loved this animal so much that I would hurry through my breakfast each morning and then rush off to find him, as by then I hadn't seen him for more than twelve hours. At the age of seven that length of time is an eternity. I was completely fascinated by him and hated being separated for very long. My father saw how fond I had become of this small, flat-faced, endearing dog and promised me, 'When we get to Canada I will buy you one.' It was, in fact, another forty-three years before I saw that breed of dog again. The animal with which I fell in love was the champion French Bulldog which had been purchased in England by Robert W. Daniel, the banker from Philadelphia, and which is referred to in *A Night to Remember,* one of the books about the tragedy written later by Walter Lord. The French Bulldog is such an uncommon breed that I think it highly unlikely there could have been more than one on the ship during that particular voyage.

After the ship had sunk and we had returned to England, I longed and longed for a little dog like that, but when I described it to people I couldn't find anyone who knew what type of dog it was. As a result, it wasn't until 1955 that I discovered the breed. A year later I was given one as a present and at long last had the pleasure of owning such an affectionate animal. The beautiful French Bulldog I eventually owned was the image of the one I had played with many years previously on the *Titanic*.

When I wasn't playing with the dog or sightseeing around the ship, my special playmate was another girl of about my own age. Her name was Nina Harper and she was particularly fond of my large teddy bear which my father had bought from the middle of the Christmas display at Gamages' large store in Holborn only a few months previously. We must have made quite a spectacle for the other passengers as we dragged this big teddy bear with us all over the ship. Our thoughts as children on board the *Titanic* were a long way away from disaster and tragedy as we happily made teddy the centre of our games together.

Nina was on her way to the USA with her father, a Glasgow minister, and her aunt. The Reverend John Harper died in the disaster along with my father and many other passengers, but Nina and her aunt survived and returned to Scotland. Because Nina and I had become such good friends my mother tried to trace her after we returned to England, but had no success. It was sixty-five years before I was eventually able to re-establish contact with Nina as a result of a newspaper article about her that someone sent me. She was still living in Scotland and like me had not talked about the disaster for many years. We kept up a correspondence until she died in the late 1980s, but did not have a chance to meet again.

In the daytime when father and I were enjoying ourselves around the ship, my mother caught up on her sleep. So, during those days, I did not see a great deal of her except first thing in the morning and last thing at night. She was still quite certain that something would happen to the ship and was anxious that it did not occur while we were all asleep at the same time.

On the Saturday night she had stayed up as usual and heard an odd sound which she did not associate with the normal life of the ship to which she had become accustomed. Because of this she roused my father and persuaded him to go on deck to find out what it was. When he came back he was rather annoyed and said, 'Oh, don't ask me to do that again. I felt so foolish when I bumped into one of the officers and he wanted to know what I was doing up there. All I could say was that my wife had heard something odd. So don't make me feel such a fool again.'

Despite this rebuke she insisted upon being told what had caused the noise she had heard. Very reluctantly, he told her it was pack ice and that she had heard the ice against the side of the ship as it went through the ice field. At the same time he said, 'We're going at a devil of a rate!'

This particular incident occurred nearly twenty-four hours before the ship foundered. Although official reports of the maiden voyage of the *Titanic* do not refer to the ship passing through an ice field on the Saturday night, my mother always insisted that was the explanation for the noise she had heard on the side of the ship. I certainly remember that the following morning when we were at breakfast together we noticed that the temperature was much colder than it had been. And during the meal, several people came over to our table and asked my mother if she had heard the noise during the night. When she said she had, one of the male passengers confirmed that it had been ice. This did nothing to calm her apprehension at being on the ship. No doubt she would have been even more worried if she had known that the normal boat drill had been dispensed with on the *Titanic*.

After we had eaten and were leaving the dining room, she saw a notice pinned on the green baize board inside the door of the dining room informing passengers of a church service later in the morning. So instead of going to bed, as she had done on other mornings, she stayed up and attended the 11.00 a.m. service, held in the dining room after it had been cleared.

As it was near to lunch time when the service finished, my mother decided that on this occasion she would stay up and join us for lunch. Because of this, my father made quite a party of it, not knowing it would actually be the last family meal with the three of us together. I later obtained a facsimile of the menu of that last meal that we had. It was of a very high standard, as would be expected on a luxury Atlantic liner. It included Chicken Maryland, salmon, ox tongue and a wide range of cheeses. We were certainly well fed that Sunday.

One of the ship's officers was particularly pleased to see us all together at lunch and came over to speak to mother. 'Does this mean that now we are getting across the Atlantic you have got over your fears?' he asked. 'Have you finished sitting up guarding us at night-time?' The remark was not intended unkindly, but no member of a ship's crew is anxious to have passengers who are worried about the safety of the ship, as this can upset other passengers on board.

'Oh no, I'm going to bed now' she replied.

The officer patted her on the shoulder and said light-heartedly, 'Ah, well, we shall be quite safe if you look after us again tonight.'

Many years later, that same officer reminded me of the conversation he had had at our lunch table, as he was one of the survivors who lived to see the making of the film *A Night to Remember*.

After our very satisfying lunch, the three of us went to the library to rest for a short time before mother left us to go to bed. She took the opportunity to write a letter to her own mother back in Chadwell Heath. It was intended that the letter would stay with the ship to be delivered on its return journey. As it was, it was never mailed and survived the disaster with the two of us. I kept it for many years until I agreed to it being auctioned at Christie's in London on the 8oth anniversary of the disaster. The new owner was kind enough to send me some good quality photographs after she added the letter to her extensive collection of *Titanic* memorabilia.

Writing on note paper embossed with the White Star Line flag and headed 'On board RMS *Titanic*', my mother makes it very clear that she was not enjoying the trip at all. She gave a very lucid picture of life on the ship through her worried eyes. That Sunday afternoon she wrote:

My Dear ones all,
As you see it is Sunday afternoon and we are resting in the library after luncheon. I was very bad all day yesterday could not eat or drink and sick all the while, but today I have got

over it. This morning Eva and I went to church and she was so pleased they sang *'Oh God our help in ages past,* that is her Hymn she sang so nicely. So she sang out loudly she is very bonny. She has had a nice ball and a box of toffee and a photo of this ship bought her today. Everybody takes notice of her through the Teddy Bear. There is to be a concert on board tomorrow night in aid of the Sailors' Home and she is going to sing so am I. Well, the sailors say we have had a wonderful passage up to now. There has been no tempest, but God knows what it must be when there is one. This mighty expanse of water, no land in sight and the ship rolling from side to side is being wonderful. Tho they say this Ship does not roll on account of its size. Any how it rolls enough for me, I shall never forget it. It is very nice weather but awfully windy and cold. They say we *may* get into New York Tuesday night but we are really due early on Wednesday morning, shall write as soon as we get there. This letter won't leave the ship but will remain and come back to England where she is due again on the 26th. Where you see the letter all of a screw is where she rolls and shakes my arm. I am sending you on a menu to show you how we live. I shall be looking forward to a line from somebody to cheer me up a bit. I am always shutting my eyes and I see everything as left it. I hope you are all quite well. Let this be an all round letter as I can't write properly to all 'till I can set my foot on shore again. We have met some nice people on board, Lucy, and so it has been nice so far. But oh the long, long days and nights. It's the longest break I ever spent in my life. I must close now with all our fondest love to all of you.

From your loving Ess

Mother left enough space for me to add my own message written in my large immature letters saying:

heaps of love and kisses to all from Eva.

Little did we think at the time that we would eventually bring the letter back to England ourselves.

It was quite clear from the message that the journey was a terrible strain to her and she was worried all the time. There was no doubt that she needed her rest and sleep after writing it.

Following her, now normal, timetable, mother got up from bed again on Sunday in order to join father for dinner. By this time I was already asleep in my bunk cuddling my favourite doll. Mother and father's last meal together on board the ship was, like lunch, outstanding in its selection. Strangely enough, it was the menu for that meal in the second class that Walter Lord reproduced in his book [See the Bibliography]. It included curried chicken, spring lamb or roast turkey as the main dishes of the five courses.

After dinner, my father apparently became very annoyed. He and mother had gone for their usual short after-dinner stroll around the promenade deck of the ship, and everywhere they went there was gambling of some form or another going on. He had a tremendous aversion to gambling of any sort because his own father had been a compulsive gambler. As a result, he had seen what a detrimental effect gambling can have on a person. During that walk around the ship he saw sweepstakes being run and all sorts of books being made on the marvellous progress of the *Titanic* across the Atlantic. Although there was no possibility of capturing the Blue Riband, the ship had gone more than 500 miles in one day – still going at a devil of a rate. As a result, the passengers were wagering on almost everything – how far we had gone in a day, how near land we were, and what time we would dock.

This all annoyed him intensely, so that he said, 'I can't stand all this gambling. I'm reading an interesting book so I shall go to bed early and read.' So, with me tucked up and asleep in bed already and my father lying in his bunk reading, my mother continued her lonely, self-imposed vigil into the night of Sunday, 14 April 1912, reading in the chair by the side of my bunk and all the time waiting and listening, knowing that something was going to happen to that majestic liner.

3

DEATH OF A LINER

The passengers did not know that the *Titanic* had been receiving radio reports of ice fields and icebergs during the whole of Sunday. What we did know was that the ship was travelling at full speed and that this led some of the passengers to believe that we might arrive at New York earlier than previously expected. It had also caused a flurry of interest in the sweepstakes being made on the Atlantic crossing of the ship. This is, of course, a standard activity in ocean-going liners and is one way of getting the passengers interested in the practical details of the ship's progress. It was also the activity which had so angered my father, irrespective of how rapidly he was approaching his destination.

However, the *Titanic* received at least seven radio warnings on the Sunday informing her of the perils of the ice that lay ahead. Despite this, her Captain kept her going at 22 ½ knots through the clear starlit night as the air and water became colder and colder.

As the ship ploughed her way through the calm Atlantic waters on that cold night, most of her passengers had made their way to their cabins to sleep. By this time I had been asleep for several hours and my father was asleep in his bunk, having finished the book he had been reading. But as the night drew on my mother remained fully dressed, continuing her vigil as on previous nights.

It was about fifteen minutes to midnight when she felt a bump to the ship. It was such a little bump that she said it felt like a train jerking, and if she hadn't been wide awake it certainly wouldn't have wakened her. It was not even enough to cause her glass of orange juice to slop over. It didn't waken me and certainly didn't disturb my father. In fact, the effect of the collision varied throughout the ship and decreased in magnitude with the distance from the point of impact. In the lower part of the ship on the starboard side the collision caused some people to fall out of bed, whereas in many other parts of the ship passengers continued sleeping undisturbed.

Despite the minor nature of the 'jerk' and the false alarm of the previous night, mother immediately woke us both up and asked my father to go and find out what had happened. As he had not felt the bump he wasn't a bit pleased at being woken from a very deep sleep and was very cross at what he thought was my mother's imagination working overtime.

While he voiced his objections my mother had got me awake and had taken me out of my bunk. She started to dress me while I, too, protested very loudly, but did not progress very far. Eventually, my father with a very bad grace pulled his trousers on over his pyjamas and put on a very thick sheepskin lined coat. Then, grumbling as he did so, went out to try to find the cause of the bump.

He returned very quickly, and I can still see his white face as he came back into the cabin. He was a changed person, not the man I knew as my father, and I was so frightened I started to scream. He didn't need to say anything to my mother, she knew what had happened. She had known all the time what was going to happen and had just been waiting for what she had felt was inevitable. Without more ado, he took off his beautiful warm sheepskin lined coat, saying to her, 'You'd better put this thick coat on, you'll want it', and then changed into an ordinary overcoat for himself.

During this time her face had undergone a transformation; she too was white, her face had fallen and she was terribly worried. Although she had been prepared for some disaster, now that it had occurred all her fears of losing her happiness were right on the surface. She didn't need to ask him, 'What's happened?'

Without more ado father picked me up, took a blanket from off the bunk and wrapped it round me over the top of my nightdress which my mother had not had the opportunity to remove. 'Come along,' he said, 'we're going up on to the deck'; and without another word strode out of the cabin. Because of our walks around the ship he knew the location of the lifeboats, although

there had been no boat drill, so he headed straight for the lift
that was close to our cabin. That took us immediately to the boat
deck and as he went out on deck I said I wanted to go back and
fetch my large teddy bear, but I got the sharp reply, 'no one will
ever go back' from my father.

By this time, people were already rushing in all directions and
for what appeared to be a long time the message was circulated
that the lifeboats would not be launched. I remember one of the
sailors saying, 'Well, even if we did launch them and put you in
the boats, you'd be back on board for breakfast'. He obviously
had no concept of the degree of damage the ship had sustained,
although part of the iceberg had broken off and left several tons
of ice on the decks. No doubt during this delay the Captain was
having the real extent of the damage assessed.

What none of us knew at this stage was that the iceberg had
torn a narrow gash some 300 feet long below the waterline on
the starboard side of the ship. What was even worse was that this
gash extended along five of the sixteen watertight compartments
in the bottom of the ship and these were rapidly filling with
water. Despite everything that had been said about the *Titanic*
being unsinkable the truth of the matter was that she could float
if any two of the sixteen compartments were flooded or if the first
four compartments were flooded. But there was no possible hope
of her floating if five compartments were breached because the
amount of water in those compartments would be sufficient to
cause the bow of the ship to dip enough to cause the water from
the fifth compartment to pour over the bulkhead into the sixth,
as these were not self-contained and totally enclosed sections.
Eventually, when the sixth compartment was partially full, the
slope of the ship would cause the water to pour into the seventh
and so on until there was enough water to sink the ship. It was
only as a result of the engineers keeping the engines going in
order to work the pumps that the ship stayed afloat as long as
she did.

After we had been standing around for some little time, my
father became very apprehensive. He knew a great deal about
the sea because he was a native of Hull and had been brought up
in what was then a mainly fishing community. He had also been
to sea a great deal during his life and had an understanding and
feel for ships. His first action on deck had been to place us close
to one of the lifeboats. 'Now stay right here and don't move' he
said to my mother, who was keeping a very tight hold of me. 'I'm

going off to see what they are going to do and whether or not they are going to launch these lifeboats.'

We were on the port side at the middle of the ship, where lifeboats No. 10, 12, 14 and 16 were hanging on their davits. We waited anxiously for his return from the quest for information. During this time more and more people were coming on deck, but apparently many were still staying in their cabins and bunks, certain that the ship would not sink. Any doubts that there was any impending danger were dispelled when the passengers and crew saw the first of the emergency rockets released into the cloudless sky. Even the most ill-informed landlubber knew that rockets at sea meant that the ship was asking for help from any other vessel in the vicinity.

When he eventually returned, father was able to tell us and the other passengers round about that the lifeboats were going to be launched. A short time later, under the supervision of the ship's officers, loading of the boats started. During the course of loading we saw some frantic pushing and shoving by people now anxious to get off the *Titanic* as fast as possible. Fifth Officer Lowe, who was directing the filling of our lifeboat, drew his revolver and fired a shot into the air, shouting, 'if anybody tries to get here in front of women and children I'll shoot'. And nobody had any doubt that he meant what he said. I heard my father say, 'I'm not trying to get in, but for God's sake look after my wife and child'. He then made sure we were safely in boat No. 14 and then continued to help other mothers and children climb in to fill it up before he stepped back.

As the lifeboat was being filled with people, we could feel that the deck of the *Titanic* was sloping more and more as the water rushed into the holds. There was a great deal of activity in the rest of the ship during this time and throughout it all we could hear the piercing shriek of steam being released from the boilers. While the lifeboats were being loaded the wireless operators were sending out the emergency signals: MGY (the call sign for the *Titanic)* and CQD (the Marconi signal for distress) followed by the position of the ship, which was given as 41° 46' N, 50° 14' W. The CQD signal (– • – • / – – • – / – • •) which stood for Come Quick, Danger, was first employed on 23 January 1909 when the *Republic,* a White Star liner, collided with the *Florida* of the Lloyd Italiano line. The signal from the *Republic* was the first distress-at-sea signal relayed by a Marconi receiving station. The SOS signal (• • • / – – – / • • •) was actually created as early as 1906 by the International Radio and Telegraphic Convention in Berlin and was introduced as it was easy to remember and quicker to transmit, particularly for an amateur.

A little later, in addition to the CQD signal, the Marconi Marine operators used the internationally adopted emergency signal, SOS, and the *Titanic* again made history that night by being the first White Star liner to radio the SOS signal.

A large number of ships acknowledged the signals and turned to help. It must have been a great shock for many of those ships' captains to receive signals from the largest ship in the world asking for help on its maiden voyage. It is easy to understand why the initial reaction in some instances was to believe it was a leg-pull. But the response was immediate, a large number of ships followed their acknowledgements of the signals by turning to give what aid they could. Some were over 200 miles away and needed to steam for more than a day to reach the stricken liner, but they still changed course just in case there was nothing nearer. The nearest ship that received the emergency radio message and turned towards the *Titanic* was the Cunard liner *Carpathia*. She was 58 miles to the south-east when the signal was picked up at 00.25 a.m. (Monday morning), about forty minutes after the *Titanic* had struck the iceberg.

As the *Titanic* was slowly sinking the officers on watch could see another ship only a few miles away. Although there has always been some argument about the identity of that particular ship it has often been claimed that it was the Leyland steamer, *Californian*. The *Titanic* had been warned of the ice field by the *Californian* earlier on Sunday; now that ship was stationary somewhere in the same area, waiting for daybreak before finding a safe route out of the ice. Although she was unable to receive the radio signals asking for help, because her only radio operator was off duty and asleep, members of the crew of the *Californian* did see rocket signals released from the deck of a nearby ship. Irrespective of whether or not there were other ships in our vicinity, I have always held the view that the *Californian* should have responded to that appeal for help after seeing the emergency rockets. Even if she had been 20 miles or more away, as has frequently been claimed, she could still have reached the *Titanic* before she sank, and long before the *Carpathia* arrived there. Possibly my father and some of the 1,500 other people need not have died if only help had arrived a lot earlier than it did.

I am in no position to say whether or not it was the *Californian* that the officers actually saw from the deck of our sinking ship and which failed to help when we most needed it. However, I do know that from the lifeboat I was in, myself and the other survivors could see another ship on the horizon. We all wondered why it did not come to assist us. The question of the identity of the mysterious ship may never be fully resolved as the claims and counter-claims depend very much on the reliability of figures for longitude and latitude written into the various ships' logs. This uncertainty about the locations of the various ships involved in the saga was very clearly illustrated many years later by Robert Ballard in his book *The Discovery of the Titanic.* The inaccuracies in the recorded positions were probably major reasons why the wreck took longer to find than expected, during the underwater searches many years later.

While we waited on the boat deck we all became conscious of music being played close at hand by a group of musicians. There has always been a great deal of argument about whether or not this story is apocryphal or total fabrication. Obviously, in a ship that large not everyone would hear a group of musicians above the noise of released steam, and it is not surprising that survivors from the starboard side of the ship have denied that any music was played. There is equally no doubt that in our part of the ship those musicians did the only thing they possibly could, to help stop panic taking hold during the loading of the lifeboats. I was not really aware of what they were playing, but I do get cross with people who say they did not play *Nearer My God to Thee.* The fact that this tune was played was emphasised very strongly by Sir Philip Gibbs in *The Deathless Story of the Titanic* which was written immediately alter the disaster. The tune played actually meant very little to me at the time, but less than a year later I was in church with my grandmother when they played that particular hymn. Although I had no conscious memory of having heard it on the deck of the *Titanic* I burst into tears and it brought back nightmares of the disaster, because I then remembered where and when I had previously heard it and the whole scene was recalled for me. I have found that other survivors who have disagreed with me on this point were usually in a different section of the ship and so were unlikely to have heard the musicians playing.

Eventually our lifeboat was ready for lowering down the side of the stricken liner and we could see over to the smooth, cold, black water below. As our boat was ready to drop my father said,

'Stay with your mummy and hold her hand tightly like a good girl'. My mother held me closely to her as we took what was to be a last look at my father before we dropped below the level of the boat deck. I didn't know that I was never going to see him again.

4

ADRIFT IN THE ATLANTIC

The lowering of the lifeboat was itself a hair-raising experience. As the boat deck of the ship was at least 70 feet above the water level it was equivalent to being lowered down the side of a 9- or 10-storey building in a series of sharp jerks as the ropes were paid out from the davits. But eventually we were in the water, which remained unusually smooth and still. Then we were rowed away from the ship to wait with the others, while it sank lower and lower at the bow. At this stage few passengers were aware that there were insufficient lifeboats and many women thought their husbands would probably get another lifeboat after all the women and children had left. But the chance of survival for anyone left on the ship was to be slim.

Before the *Titanic* sank we could clearly hear the noise of people shouting and screaming on board, and I can only assume that there was some panic amongst the passengers and crew who had come onto the boat deck only to find that all the lifeboats had gone and they had no hope of avoiding the freezing cold water with its almost certain death. There has, of course, been a great deal of conjecture as to what took place on the ship as she actually went down. Those of us who were in the lifeboats were 200 or 300 yards away at least and were in no position to pontificate on the conduct or behaviour of 1,500 people, all of whom were facing death through no fault of their own but because of the stupidity and shortsightedness of others. Only a handful of those left on board survived to tell the tale. In a few cases they were picked up by partially filled lifeboats, while others were saved by climbing on to the bottom of an inverted Engelhardt which it had not been possible to launch properly.

The lifeboat into which we had been placed by my father was heavily laden, probably beyond its specified capacity, and when we reached the water the officer in charge had it rowed well clear of the *Titanic* to avoid the expected drag or wash when the ship finally sank. Nobody had any clear idea at that stage as to how many people were still on board the ship or even if all the lifeboats had been launched. But we could see other lifeboats on the water around us, all staying well clear of the liner as she slipped lower and lower at the bow.

And so we waited, with the clear sky above and the calm, cold sea around, with icebergs 300 feet high clearly visible in the starlight and reflecting the lights from the ship. Slowly, very slowly, we could see the *Titanic* getting lower in the water. As the slope of the decks became even greater there was an increasing amount of noise, from the people still on board, from loose articles sliding along the decks and from the boilers as they eventually tore loose from the ship's body and fell through the length of the hull. Then, for a short time, she seemed to hang almost vertically as if suspended from the sky with her stem clearly above the water. We all seemed to hold our breaths for what we knew would be the end of that fabulous liner that had been our home for just a few days.

It appeared to me then that she broke in half before the stern slid slowly, steadily, even gracefully, to follow the bow below the surface of the calm Atlantic ocean. Many times after the event I was told that the *Titanic* couldn't have broken in two and must have sunk in one piece, but I was always certain she had. Eventually I was proved correct when the wreck was discovered in two distinct parts by Bob Ballard's expedition many years later. With the sinking ship went the hopes and aspirations of hundreds of people, their lives cut short through man's presumption.

Because of the great sacrifice made by the engineers in keeping the pumps working the ship had stayed afloat much longer than many people had expected. As a result it was 2.20 a.m., over two and a half hours after striking the iceberg, before the *Titanic* finally sank from sight, eventually coming to lie on the sea bed at a depth of 2,077 fathoms (2.4 miles, or 3.8 kilometres).

The horror of seeing that incredible ship sink was unbelievable. One minute the ship was there with its lights still ablaze and illuminating the sea all around, and the next minute it was gone and the only light was from the stars. At the same time there was a great noise from the screams and cries of hundreds of people plunged into the penetratingly cold, icy, Atlantic with little hope of being saved. For the first time we all fully realised that there had been many people left on the ship without access to lifeboats and that they were now doomed. My father was a champion swimmer and in warmer water could have remained afloat a long time, but he was not a fat man and probably succumbed very quickly to the coldness of the water. I have always been haunted by the thought that he must have tried, despite the intense cold, to swim for his life to reach a lifeboat. But few people survived for more than a few minutes in the icy water and most of those actually pulled from the sea died from exposure before morning. The survivors in the lifeboats who lived to see and hear it all could never forget the agony and tragedy of the drama that was played out in front of them. It engraved itself upon our minds and lived with us all.

When the *Titanic* had gone, those in charge started to try and collect the lifeboats into groups. This was not an easy thing to do as they had become well scattered from where the ship had been and only two or three of the sixteen main lifeboats actually had any lights. But eventually some of the boats did manage to come together and our particular boat was in a group of about four or five. It was then realised that a number of the lifeboats had left the *Titanic* before being completely filled. This fact has often been criticised in reports and books published since the disaster, but it is important to realise that when the first lifeboats were being lowered many passengers would not get into them, mainly because they were not convinced that the ship was sinking and they did not want to spend the night on the sea in a small boat unnecessarily. Unfortunately, some of the lightly laden boats had been rowed some considerable distance from the sinking liner to avoid any undertow when she finally went down. As a result, they were poorly placed to pick up survivors from the water before they died from the cold.

My mother and I were initially in lifeboat No. 14 which, with sixty passengers, was the most heavily laden boat from the port side. This made it unsuitable for picking up any additional survivors. But in our group of lifeboats one of the officers took command and made himself responsible for redistributing the survivors between them in order to make one boat almost completely empty to pick up people still swimming in the water.

The officer called over to each boat in turn, 'How many can you take?' They in their turn called back, 'We can take three in this boat', another said, 'Well, we can manage to take another six', whilst a third replied, 'We can't take any, we're already overcrowded'. So, there in the middle of the Atlantic Ocean early on that Monday morning, we went through the ghastly experience of being trans-shipped in the dark from one lifeboat to another while people were crying and dying around us. That type of activity is hazardous at the best of times and was particularly difficult and slow to carry out under the conditions we were enduring.

Eventually, the officer in charge managed to reduce the numbers in our lifeboat, and he clearly considered that our safety was his first priority. The lifeboat was then able to return to seek other survivors from where the *Titanic* had sunk. But the transferring of survivors had taken a long time during which the cries for help subsided from the water which was at a temperature of 28°F (-2°C). We later learnt that this particular boat only managed to pick up an additional four survivors. It is easy to see now that it would have been better if some of the half-empty boats had been taken back immediately by the more experienced sailors, as they would not have had to waste time transferring passengers, but it was a brave attempt that was mainly defeated by the very cold conditions.

Due to a combination of coldness and fright I had been clinging as firmly as possible to my mother, who was still very cold despite the sheepskin coat she had been made to put on. At the same time I was pulling my blanket tightly around myself, as much for security as for warmth. But we became involved in the mid-Atlantic trans-shipment which was being carried out between the lifeboats. The result of this was that somehow we became separated. How this occurred we could never work out, but separated we were. To me, that really was the most terrifying thing of all. I had already been parted from my father when we left the ship, although I had not realised at that stage that I wouldn't see him again. Now I had also been parted from my mother. It was bad enough going through what I had, without being deprived of the only remaining person who was the centre of what was left of my world. So I started screaming for her, and no doubt added to the level of misery around me. I cried and cried, on and off throughout the whole of the remainder of the night; somebody else tried to comfort me during that time but I never knew who she was. My mother, for her part, was panic stricken when she found I was not in the same boat. She kept trying to find out into which lifeboat I had been transferred, but had no success. It was not until we had all been picked up that we found each other, many hours later.

From where we were on the water we could see the lights of that other ship some miles away. We all hoped she had seen the rockets released before the *Titanic* sank, but as we watched she made no movement towards us and the feelings of despair amongst the poor souls in the lifeboats can well be imagined. Some of the survivors in other lifeboats tried to row towards the ship, but she was too far away to be easily reached. It was not until the inquiries into the disaster were completed that we learnt that the stationary ship was thought to be the *Californian.*

Doubt about the true identity of that ship still exists even after all this time. Captain Lord of the *Californian,* and his family, spent many years trying to clear his name of the blame that was later heaped upon him. But, despite the findings of several inquiries, the most recent one being in Great Britain that reported in 1991, the doubts continue. Captain Lord always claimed that his ship was further away from the *Titanic* than was originally believed and that what his crew saw were company flares, rather than rockets. I still wonder how many ships were firing coloured lights into the sky within 20 miles of the *Californian* on that particular cold Atlantic winter's night. The *Californian* did arrive to help at 8.00 a.m. that morning, after the *Carpathia* had picked up all the survivors.

But for those of us in the lifeboats the cold night dragged on, with some people quietly sitting keeping their thoughts, fears and losses to themselves. Others were clasping their children trying to keep them warm, some were weeping as they thought of relations or friends they had lost, and some were talking and starting the post-mortem on the ship, which was go to on for many years. Few people had managed to bring any possessions with them. All sat there hoping that either the rocket signals had been seen or that the radio signals had been heard by a ship near enough to pick us up, before we too slowly froze to death in those small boats.

During this time, unknown to us, the *Carpathia* was steaming at its full speed of 17 ½ knots through the same ice field which had been the cause of sinking our much bigger ship. During its 58 mile rescue dash through the night, Captain Arthur H. Rostron had his ship prepared to take on survivors. Blankets were laid out in the diningroom and library, hot food was prepared, ladders were hung down the ship's side, and doorways opened, all in readiness to get people on board with the minimum of delay. Most of the passengers on the *Carpathia* were unaware of these preparations, at least until they realised they were steaming rapidly through the ice field. The ship had been outward bound from New York and mainly contained

US citizens, former immigrants from Italy and the Balkan states, who were on their way to Europe for vacations in their countries of origin. As it was, those vacations were to be much delayed when the *Cmpathia* later turned back to New York with its additional load of unexpected passengers.

Despite the great risk of a collision, Captain Rostron maintained his ship's high speed for as long as possible and, with lookouts warning the bridge of icebergs every few minutes, steered a safe route through the ice field. Some years later, the then knighted, Sir Arthur H. Rostron wrote his biography *Home From the Sea* and told his story of the race through the ice to reach the *Titanic* survivors. He related how it was only because of a conscientious wireless operator, the only one on board, working a little late and stopping to unlace his boots that the signal from the *Titanic* was picked up by the *Carpathia*. As a result, 706 people were actually picked up, although one man later died on board the *Carpathia*. But I often shudder to think of the extra hours we would have spent in those cold boats waiting for the SOS to be answered by other ships further away.

As dawn broke over the cold sea at about 4.00 a.m. that April morning, we could see the lifeboats ringed about by huge icebergs as far as the horizon. Between two of these huge, jagged peaks we saw what appeared at first to be a very small ship moving steadily towards us. All this time the sea had been calm and smooth, but now as the day brightened we could feel a swell beginning to develop. So we were overwhelmed with relief at the sight of just that one ship which offered hope of warmth and comfort to those of us who had survived the ordeal. The *Carpathia* started to pick up the survivors as quickly as possible, but it was a long job and some of the lifeboats had to row three or four miles to reach her. Our boat must have been one of the last to be cleared as it was about 8.30 a.m. before I was actually on board the ship. The adults had to climb up vertical rope ladders which hung down the side of the ship. But that was too terrifying for the younger children. We were almost hysterical with fright at this new terror of having to get from the surface of the ocean back up the side of a ship. Because of this a different procedure was used. We were each put into a large canvas bag with our heads poking out at the top, and several 'bags' were then put into a lifting net which was winched up very quickly by a wheel on the deck. And so we arrived wet, cold and frightened amongst the wondering crew and passengers of the *Carpathia*. I was more frightened by this experience than by almost anything else that happened in the whole of those tragic events.

As soon as we were on board we were taken below to one of the big rooms where we were each wrapped in a big, dry blanket and given something hot to drink. I remember having all sorts of odd clothes piled around me, including a man's coat. All this time my mother was frantically searching everywhere for me, hoping that I would be on the ship somewhere. By now the ship was very congested and finding anyone was not easy as the number of passengers had doubled in a matter of a few hours. As a result there were throngs of people in all the companionways.

While I was still crying for my mother, between dozing and being comforted by strangers, she was going from one part of the ship to another asking everyone she could if they had seen me. It was much later in the day before she discovered me, still miserable and huddled under borrowed clothing. We clung to each other with tears of relief, sharing our suffering and gaining much comfort from being together again. I have never forgotten what it was like to feel that I might have lost both my parents in that tragedy. To be an orphan at a young age must be a heartbreaking experience for any child, and I have always been grateful that I did have one parent at least to guide me and see me grow up. She didn't let me out of her sight for the rest of the journey to New York.

The *Carpathia* was a much smaller and slower ship than the *Titanic* and only had a single funnel. But, despite her size and lack of speed, she was paradise after the exposure and bleakness of the lifeboats. She gave us warmth, comfort and dryness; above all, she gave us back life and hope. We would never forget the *Carpathia* and the risks that were taken to come to our aid.

The people on board that ship couldn't have been kinder to us. Some of them were immigrants to the USA who had been turned back at Ellis Island; many of them were naturalised US citizens returning to Europe on vacation. Despite this severe disruption to their own plans, and although many of them were fairly poor, they still found us articles of clothing. In some cases they gave up their cabins to the survivors and at all times they did their best to comfort and help us.

Although some of the *Titanic* survivors were fortunate enough to be given empty cabins on the *Carpathia,* most of us had to sleep in either the dining saloon or the library on straw mattresses. My bed was made up on one of the dining tables. Apart from food, warmth and sleep, some people needed to have medical attention for frostbite. Mother and I had both suffered from the exposure. Despite my father's foresight in giving mother his coat, most of our clothing had been inadequate against the penetrating damp and cold. The blanket had helped prevent me from suffering serious injury, but I did have partially frostbitten ears and a more badly frostbitten toe. Fortunately, I recovered from these within a few days. But a lot of the other survivors who had just thrown light coats or thin dressing-gowns over the top of their night-clothes had suffered very badly during the cold wait. The ship's doctor had a great deal of work to do because, in addition to the cases of frostbite, he had patients who had been injured getting into the lifeboats and a number suffering from shock.

The rescue had really come only just in time. Shortly after the *Carpathia* picked us up the weather deteriorated and by the afternoon of that day was quite bad. It took Captain Rostron four hours to navigate his ship out of the ice-field again, and then we ran into a most dreadful fog. Every few minutes we had the monotonous blaring of the fog horn in our ears while the wet, clammy fog swirled around us. The ship could make only very slow progress. Then, as if we had not suffered enough – as if the sea was loath to lose its prey – the fog was followed by a frightful thunder storm. It was almost as if the Atlantic was doing its worst to claim the few survivors who remained from what had been the *Titanic*. Our new ship was unable to go very fast under these appalling conditions. She was relatively slow in any case and now she was heavily overladen. So she slowly limped back to New York with 706 survivors, while the remains of that wonderful ship and many of her 1,502 dead lay in the depths of the Atlantic. The published figures for those who survived vary from 651 to 711, and for those who died from 1,490 to 1,517. After all these years it is difficult to obtain complete accuracy, but Geoffrey Marcus's figures relate closely to those from the Board of Trade and those recorded by Lawrence Beesley.

It was not until a day or so after the tragedy that any form of a survivors' list was available for publication in newspapers in the USA or Great Britain, although news of what had occurred rapidly made the headlines throughout the world. The initial lists produced were based upon names taken from us and radioed as rapidly as possible from the *Carpathia*. These lists were incomplete, as well as being partially incorrect. The full magnitude of the loss of life was not appreciated until we docked at New York. Many relatives and friends who had waited anxiously over the days had their hopes dashed to the ground and found their worst fears fulfilled. Although one third of the passengers and crew actually survived, we later found out that the smallest proportion of survivors was amongst the men in the second class – only thirteen lived out of the 160 on the ship.

Of the second class passengers all twenty-four children survived and seventy-eight of the ninety-three women. Nobody has ever satisfactorily explained why so few of the men survived – it may have been old world gallantry of 'women and children first', but that does not explain how a larger proportion of the men from the third class found room in the lifeboats. It is another of the many unanswered questions about the *Titanic* disaster.

Those of us who had survived knew we owed our lives to the invention of Guglieimo Marconi which had been in use for only a few years. Without it there could well have been no survivors at all as we could not have lasted very long in those cold temperatures and would probably have had our lifeboats sunk by the storm which followed. Without the radio it would have been another two or three days before our loss would have been known and vessels could have been sent to search for us, especially as our emergency rockets had been ignored. Marconi's first transatlantic broadcast had taken place only eleven years earlier, from Signal Hill, Newfoundland on 12 December 1901. By 1912 it had it had become standard practice to have wireless operators on all ships but, not necessarily with a twenty-four hour service.

5

EVA'S MOTHER'S ACCOUNT

Esther Hart gave an interview to her local newspaper the *Ilford Graphic* which ran the story on 12 May 1912. It was titled 'The tale of the *Titanic* told by a rescued Ilford lady: Mrs Ben Hart's (Esther Hart) personal and thrilling narrative'. The article came to light after Eva Hart died but is inserted in her memoir to give her mother's perspective on events. Apart from the odd inconsistency the two accounts are very similar, but new details emerge.

> I can honestly say that from the moment the journey to Canada was mentioned, till the time we got aboard the *Titanic*, I never contemplated with any other feelings but those of dread and uneasiness. It was all done in a hurry. My husband of late had not been successful in business and things looked like going from bad to worse.
>
> He was a very clever carpenter and his chest of tools was considered to be as perfect and expensive as any carpenter could wish for. At any rate he valued them at £100. He was going out to start building with a Mr Wire at Winnipeg. Mr Wire has since written to me expressing his deep regret at Ben's untimely loss, and adding, 'There were five Winnipeg men lost on the *Titanic* and I might have been one of them.'
>
> The idea seized on Ben's imagination. 'I'll go out to a new country,' he said, 'where I'll either sink or swim.' In fact, during

the time prior to our leaving Ilford, the latter statement was always in his mouth. I little knew then how sadly prophetic it was to turn out for my poor dear.

I said at the commencement that I viewed the journey with dread and uneasiness, but in saying that I do not wish anyone to think that I ever imagined anything so dreadful would happen as did happen. You see I was leaving my father and mother when they were at fairly advanced age, and neither of them in the best of health and I knew that in saying goodbye, I was saying goodbye forever: but it has pleased God to take my husband and send me back to them. Then I was leaving all the friends I had known in Ilford for so many years: and lastly, I dreaded the sea: the idea of being on the sea at night was bad enough, but for six or seven, I could not contemplate it, it was a nightmare to me.

Well, we said all our 'Goodbyes' and reached Southampton, and almost the first thing Ben did was take me to see the *Titanic*. He was always an enthusiastic in anything he was interested in: and he could not have been more enthusiastic over the *Titanic* had he been a part proprietor of it. 'There, old girl,' he said, 'there's a vessel for you! You're not afraid now.' I tried to share his confidence, but my heart quite failed me when we got aboard and I counted the number of boats there were. I said, 'Ben, we are carrying over 2,000 people and there are not enough boats for half of them if anything happens.' He laughed at my fears and said that beyond boat drills he did not expect the boats would come off the davits. But from that moment I made up my mind to one thing, till we were safe on land at New York. Nothing should ever persuade me to undress, and nothing did, although Ben at times got very cross with me. So each night I simply rested in my bunk, fully dressed and fully prepared, God knows why, for the worst.

We were fortunate in having some very nice people at our table. We were in parties of eight in the second saloon, and our party included a lady and gentleman from the Cape, Mr and Mrs Brown and their daughter, who were on their way to Vancouver. Mr Guggenheim's (a millionaire) chauffeur (both Mr and Mrs Guggenheim and he were drowned), a lady named Mrs Mary Mack, whose body has since been recovered, and Mr Hart, myself, and baby.

Mr Brown and Ben got on capitally together. They were the exact opposite of each other. Mr Brown was a quiet, reserved man who scarcely ever spoke, and Ben was fond of talking and so they got on well, promenaded the deck together, had their midday 'Bass' together, and smoked their pipes together. Indeed, Mrs Brown said that she had never seen her husband 'take' to anyone like he had to my Ben.

Oh dear! Oh dear! To think that, of the eight at the table, four were taken and four were left. I can see their bright, happy faces now as we sat round that table at meal times, talking of the future; they were all so confident, so looking forward to a new life in a new land, and well they found it, but in God's way, not theirs.

Now a very curious thing happened on the Saturday night. We had made splendid progress, and although I was still far from easy in my mind, I was as content as I could be off the land. I heard someone remark with glee that we were making a beeline for New York. I knew we were going at a tremendous speed, and it was the general talk – I cannot say what truth there was in it – that the captain and officers were 'on' something good if we broke the record.

But on the Saturday night I was resting in my bunk and my husband was sound asleep above me. Everything was quiet, except the throb of the screw and a strange straining and creaking of everything in the cabin, which I had noticed all the voyage. I may have just dozed off when I was awakened by a feeling as if some gigantic force had given the ship a mighty push behind. I could even hear the swirl of the waters which such a push to such a vessel would cause. I sat up, no doubt as to my being wide awake, again came the push and the swirl, and yet again a third time. For a few minutes I was dazed, frozen with terror of I know not what. Then I stood up and shook my husband, who was still sleeping soundly. 'Ben,' I said, 'Ben, wake up, get up, something dreadful has happened or is going to happen.' He was a little cross, as a man naturally is when he is woken from a sound sleep by the ungrounded fears (as he thinks) of a woman, but he saw that I was upset, and so he got up and partly dressed, and went up on the hurricane deck, and soon returned and assured me that the sea was calm and that the ship was travelling smoothly.

The next morning at breakfast, he laughingly told our table about it, and said what he was going to do that (Sunday) night to keep me quiet. He was going to insist upon my having a strong glass of hot grog to make me sleep. Mr Brown explained the creaking and straining by saying that as it was a new vessel everything was settling down into its proper place. 'Why,' he said. 'When we get to New York, it's more than likely that a lot of the paint will have come away, a lot of the joints have started,' and so on. 'That's all very well,' I said, 'but what about those awful jerks one after the other?' That he could not explain, nor anybody else. I say it was a warning from God to me, for I think that perhaps I was the only one of the 2,000 odd about who went in daily and nightly dread of the unforeseen. But had I told it to those in authority! Would anyone have listened to a silly, weak woman's superstitious fears? Would they have gone one hair's breadth out of their course? Would they have ordered one revolution less per minute of the screw? So I could only do what women have had to do from the beginning, eat my heart out with fear and wait.

Now if I had known that just at this time of the year the icebergs get across the track of the Atlantic liners, a little incident which occurred on this Sunday would have sent me straight to the captain, even if I'd have had to climb on to his bridge. But the simple things we ought to know we are never told. My husband was always a man who could bear extremes of heat and cold better than anyone I have ever met. All through those trying days of heat last year, when everyone else was melting and parched, he never once grumbled, but kept as cool as a cucumber. And the same with the cold. I have known him, when other people have been hanging over the fires, in and out of the house with his coat off, laughing at the poor shivering ones. And yet at midday on this fatal Sunday, he suddenly came up to baby and myself, and said rubbing his hands, 'How cold it has turned. I feel as if there was not a warm drop of blood in my body. Come and have a romp with daddy,' he said to baby, and together they went off and ran and romped on the hurricane desk.

We were in the iceberg region and the Almighty sent a warning to my husband – the man who was never cold before now shivered and shook like one stricken with ague.

But, beyond thinking it a curious thing, we took no heed.

And now, I come to a part of my story that I shrink from telling. Indeed, I think I have lingered over the first part because I dread relating the events of that awful night. I have read somewhere of people living a whole lifetime in a few hours. I know now that I have done so. To have gone through what I went through, to have suffered what I have suffered, to have seen what I have seen, to know what I know, and still to be alive, and above all – thank the Lord – to still preserve my reason, is a great and a growing marvel to me.

We had retired to our cabin about 10, and my husband, who thoroughly enjoyed the life aboard ship and drank his fill of the ozone – he could never get enough of it – was soon undressed and fast asleep in his bunk. My little Eva too was sound asleep, and I was sitting on my portmanteau with my head resting on the side of my bunk. And then all of a sudden there came the most awful sound I have ever heard in my life, a dreadful tearing and ripping sound – how any people who were awake at the time can say they scarcely felt a shock I cannot understand – the sound of great masses of steel and iron being violently torn, rent and cut asunder.

I was on my feet in an instant, for I knew something dreadful had happened. I shook Ben, and he awoke. 'Daddy,' I said, 'get up at once. We have hit something I am sure and it's serious.' Poor dear Ben! He was partly asleep still, and he said, 'Oh woman – again! I really don't know what I shall do with you?' 'Ben,' I said, not loudly, but with a quiet insistence which influenced him far more, 'something has happened; go up on deck and find out what it is.' He went up in his nightshirt and bare feet; in a few moments he was back again. He said, 'All the men are at the lifeboats – it's only a lifeboat drill.' I said, 'They don't have lifeboat drills at 11 at night. I tell you something has happened – dress quickly and let us dress the baby.' So he hurriedly put on his pants and his overcoat, put his big motor coat over me and then dressed the sleeping little girl. Just then a stewardess, with whom I was on friendly terms, came along and said she would soon find out all about it. She knew the Marconi operator and would ask him. So she went away and quickly came back saying that everything was all right. But I said, 'Everything is not all right, we have struck something and the water is coming in.' I think by this time Ben had realised, although he would not say so, that danger was ahead, for when he got up on B deck, he turned away for a few moments, and said his Jewish prayers. The next few minutes were so crowded with events, so fraught with all that matters in this world – life to a few of us, death to the majority of us – that I have no coherent recollection of what happened.

I know that there was a cry of 'She's sinking'. I heard hoarse shouts of 'Women and children first', and then from boat to boat we were hurried, only to be told, 'Already full.' Four boats we tried and at the fifth there was room. Eva was thrown in first, and I followed her. Just then, a man who had previously tried to get in succeeded in doing so, but was ordered out, and the officer fired his revolver into the air to let everyone see it was loaded, and shouted out, 'Stand back! I say, stand back! The next man who puts his foot in this boat, I will shoot him down like a dog.' Ben, who had been doing what he could to help the women and children, said quietly, 'I'm not going in, but for God's sake look after my wife and child.' And little Eva called out to the officer with the revolver, 'Don't shoot my daddy. You shan't shoot my daddy.' What an experience for a little child to go through! At the age of seven to have passed through the valley of the shadow of death. I wonder if she will ever forget it? I know I shan't, if I live for a hundred years.

So that was the last I saw of my poor lost dear – no farewell kiss, no fond word – but in a moment he had gone and we were hanging over the sea, 50 or 60 feet [*c.* 15–18 metres] above it, and then there were two or three horrible jerks as the boat was lowered from the davits and we were in the water, so crowded that we could scarcely move.

In the midst of all these stunning blows one despairing tact alone seized my thoughts: I knew, and a woman is never wrong in such matters, that I had seen the last of my Ben, and that I had lost the best and truest friend, the kindest and most thoughtful husband that ever woman had.

The officer in charge of our boat was standing on that raised part of it right at the end. We were all women and children aboard (at least I thought so then, but we were not, as I will presently tell you) and we were all crying and sobbing; and the officer said, not roughly, but I think with a kindly desire to keep our minds off the terrible time we had gone through. 'Don't cry, please don't cry. You'll have something else to do than cry; some of you will have to handle the oars. For God's sake stop crying. If I had not the responsibility of looking after you I would put a bullet through my brain.' So we got away from the ship for a safe distance, for there was no doubt now about her sinking. The front portion of her was pointing downwards and she appeared to be breaking in halves. Then with a mighty and tearing sob, as of some gigantic thing instinct with life, the front portion of her dived, for that is the only word I can use properly to describe it, dived into the sea, and the after part with a heavy list, also disappeared. And then a wonderful thing happened. Apart from the swirl of the water close to the vessel, caused by such a mass sinking, the sea was as smooth as glass; it seemed as if the Almighty, in order that as many should be saved as possible, had, with a merciful hand, smoothed and calmed the waters. For a few moments we could see everything that was happening, for, as the vessel sank, millions and millions of sparks flew up and lit everything around us. And in an instant the sea was alive with wreckage, with chairs, pillows, and rugs, benches, tables, cushions, and, strangely enough, black with an enormous mass of coffee beans. And the air was full of the awful and despairing cries of drowning men. And we were helpless to help, for we dared not go near them.

Our officer was busy shouting out till he was hoarse, 'Let all the boats keep as near together as possible. That's our only chance of being picked up. If we separate we are lost. Keep together.' An inky blackness now settled over us, and not a soul in our boat had a match; but the officer found in his pockets an electric torch, which he kept flashing, shouting out all the time, 'Keep together – it's our only chance.' The duty that the officer allotted to me was to bale the water out of the boat. While sitting there I had the impression that there was somebody near me who ought not to be there. So, when I could get my elbows free I put my hand down under the seat and touched a human form. It was a poor wretch of a man who had smuggled himself into the boat, and had sat there during all that awful time, under the seat in about six inches [*c.* 15 cm] of water. When we got him out he was so stiff he could scarcely move.

It had got a little lighter now, and our officer had collected nearly all the boats together; and he called from one to the other, 'How many in yours – how many in yours?' and then he discovered that there was room in those other boats to put the whole of our 55 in, so we were transferred to them, and the officer now collected a few seamen in his now empty boat and rowed away to see what he could find. So, with proper management another 55 people could easily have been saved. I cannot understand why, in the midst of such terrible doings, these boats left the ship without their full number of passengers; 55 precious lives lost either through selfishness or carelessness, I know not which.

It was no easy matter for me to get from one boat to the other. I am no light weight at the best of times, but now I was weak from want of sleep – weak with the terror of the night – and laden with Ben's heavy motor coat. Eva had been handed in, and I shall never forget my feelings when I saw her leave, and found myself unable to get a footing on the boat she was in. At last I managed it, how I could not tell. Eva was suffering from a violent attack of vomiting: for, when they had thrown her into the first boat from the *Titanic* she had hit her stomach on the edge of the boat. And there the poor little thing was, and I could not get near her to wipe her mouth. So there we sat the weary night through until, at eight in the morning, the *Carpathia* came on the scene. I always thought that these ship boats had to be provisioned beforehand, in view of possible accidents, but there was no water, nor were there biscuits in the boat. An oversight I suppose, but one fraught with terrible consequences had not the *Carpathia* arrived in good time.

Gradually the welcome dawn broke; and as the sun rose and we looked at where the sky and sea met, we saw one of the most wonderful sights that could be imagined. Right away there, stretching for miles and miles, there appeared what seemed to us an enormous fleet of yachts, with their glistening sails all spread. As the sun grew brighter they seemed to sparkle with innumerable diamonds. They were icebergs; and, moving slowly and majestically along all by itself, a mile or so in length, in form like the pictures of Gibraltar I have seen, was the monster iceberg, the cause of all our trouble.

And now about eight o'clock the *Carpathia* came into sight and we were all aboard by 8.30. I cannot say much of my life on board this vessel. It was no matter for a ship to take on another 700 people, many of them but lightly clad, most of them ill, and all suffering severely from shock; all was done for us that could be done, but I could neither rest nor sleep. My little Eva was still suffering from her vomiting attack and I found my hands full in nursing her; but when at night she was asleep, I could do nothing but walk the corridor, up and down, up and down, and thinking, thinking all the time. So much did I walk about at night that the kind-hearted sailors christened me The Lady of the Watch.

Well, eventually we arrived at New York. And what can I say of the kindness of the 'Women's Relief Committee', and the help they rendered us poor stranded souls. Kindness! That's but a poor word; and yet I can find no other for their intensely practical sympathy. No formulas, no questions. We had got to be helped and that quickly, and quickly they did it. In a short space of time with a speed that seemed incredible, there was a sufficiency of clothing for every destitute woman and child – my women readers will understand me when I say that everything a woman needed was there in abundance – from a blouse to a safety pin, underclothing, stays, stockings, garters, suspenders, hair pins, boots of all sizes, each pair with laces or a button hook in them as was necessary. I have never heard of such foresight. I have never experienced such real kindness. God bless the ladies of the 'Women's Relief Committee of New York', say I heartily and fervently. Why, Mrs Satterlee actually drove me in her beautiful car to the hotel where I was to stay pending my return to England, and wanted me to go to lunch with her in her house, but my heart was too full for that. She knew the reason and appreciated it like the lady she is. One touching little incident occurred before I sailed for home on the *Celtic*, and that was the receipt of a letter from little children in New Jersey. They had heard of my Eva and they sent her a dollar bill with a beautiful little letter. I don't think that bill will ever be changed, for both it and the letter will be framed.

There is but little to add. I returned on the *Celtic* with five other ladies from the *Titanic*, including Mrs Ada Clarke, of Southampton. We were treated with every kindness and consideration. A lady in the first saloon sent out word that whatever we wanted in the way of fruit, or any other delicacies not included in our menu, we were to have.

And now I have only one object in life, and that is the future of my little Eva. My lost Ben had such dreams of her future; he meant to do such things for her; and, whatever money I get, apart from the bare cost of the necessities of life, shall be devoted to her upbringing in such a way as shall realise, as far as my endeavours and finances can go, his wishes with regard to her.

6

AFTERMATH

It was late in the evening of Thursday 18 April 1912 before the heavily laden *Carpathia* berthed at the New York dockside. Thousands of onlookers had waited many hours to see the arrival of the small ship which had been responsible for the rescue. Everybody was very kind to us when we disembarked and despite the loss of all our money, passports and baggage, there were no undue delays in getting through the immigration control. My mother's first action was to send a cable to her parents in England confirming that we had been rescued and that we had arrived safely in the USA. The letter she had written that Sunday afternoon on the *Titanic* was never posted. She found it in the pocket of my father's sheepskin lined coat after we had been rescued and for her it was to remain a constant reminder of that tragic journey and of the loss of her husband.

My aunt in New York had seen our names in the list of survivors radioed from the *Carpathia* while we were still at sea, and was expecting us when we landed. We were lucky that we were able to go straight to her home to stay while we recovered from our ordeal. Mother had not met her previously because my aunt had left England to live in the USA when she was quite young, before my mother and father had met. She was very upset that after waiting all that time to see her brother again he should have died at sea in such tragic circumstances on his way to visit her.

Although we were made very welcome in New York, my mother had already started looking to the future. When asked about her plans she quite calmly said, 'Well, I don't want to stay here and I don't want to go to Canada. Now I just want to get back to my own people.' She knew that she would be unable to take on the partnership which my father had intended. She had no practical experience of the building trade and could see no point in continuing on to Canada. So we stayed in New York for a short time during which her major concern was obtaining berths on board a ship that could take us back direct to England as soon as possible. Somehow, she also managed to find the time and money to buy me a doll to replace the one that had gone down with my teddy bear when the *Titanic* sank. Although the US government set up an inquiry into the disaster, my mother was not one of those called to give evidence. As a passenger there was little she could have added to the expert evidence of the officers and to that of the chairman of the shipping line who had been on board that ill-fated voyage. But if asked, she could certainly have told the inquiry about the fiasco of the loading of the lifeboats and the transfers from one boat to another at sea. But she did carry out some enquiries of her own. She checked the cabin list and the survivor list in order to find out what had happened to the people whose cabins had been situated close to ours in order to ascertain whether or not they had reached the deck in time to be put into the available lifeboats. As far as she was able to determine, we were the only people saved from that part of the ship. Of the 277 second class passengers, 162 died with the *Titanic*. That we were saved was due solely to my mother's premonition. The point of the impact of the iceberg was about as far away from our cabin as it could have been. And, whereas it must have been sufficient to wake people who were near the bow of the ship, it actually only felt like a small bump in our part of the ship. No doubt many of the other people in our section reached the decks too late to be able to obtain a place in any of the four lifeboats on the port side which had been situated in our part of the ship.

This was the only time that she ever had a premonition and she was never able to think of any reason why she should have had such a strong pre-cognition just on that one occasion. There are many people who claim they have premonitions, but I have never met anyone who was so convinced as she was, to the extent that she was prepared to sit up every night and even to be ridiculed throughout the voyage.

This is not to say that there were not other people with premonitions about the maiden voyage of the *Titanic*. Quite a number of these have been documented in addition to a number of signs of ill-omen which people saw prior to the voyage. Their reliability has been assessed by George Behe in his book *Titanic, Psychic Forewarnings of a Tragedy*. Probably the most incredible of all the forecasts of doom was that written as a story in 1898, before the *Titanic* had even been built. It was not intended as an attempt at foretelling the future, but the author, Morgan Robertson, in his book entitled *The Wreck of the Titan* wrote a story about a large unsinkable liner which had dimensions almost identical to those of the real *Titanic*. The *Titan* in the novel sank through striking an iceberg, just as her real-life counterpart did fourteen years later. What made him write a book anticipating the future in this way nobody knows, but the parallel is uncanny. For my part I have great respect for people when they claim strongly to have a premonition, because my mother was 100 per cent accurate on the only occasion it happened to her – and it saved both our lives.

I later realised that in the long run a great deal of good came about as a result of that disaster and it is some consolation to know that over 1,500 people did not die totally in vain. The two enquiries, in the USA and in England, showed quite clearly how the accident could have been avoided in the first place, and how the toll of life could have been at least greatly reduced, if not prevented completely.

Steps were taken immediately after the accident to tighten up all the possible weaknesses in the procedures for safety at sea. It caused the Board of Trade to insist upon sufficient lifeboats for all people on board ocean-going ships, plus additional rafts and collapsible or inflatable boats. Boat drill, which had been considered unnecessary on the *Titanic,* was also made a compulsory feature on passenger liners and nowadays must be carried out within twelve hours of boarding ship.

Following the enquiries into the tragedy, the major maritime nations of that time met in London in the winter of 1913 for the first International Conference on Safety of Life at Sea. It was at this conference that all the weaknesses in the regulations which had contributed to the great loss of life in the *Titanic* disaster were discussed and analysed. One rapid result was the Merchant Shipping Act 1914, making the tighter safety standards legally enforceable. It also led to the creation of the International Ice Patrol in 1913, consisting of special ships used to track the drifting Arctic icebergs. The work of this patrol is now carried out by means of jet aircraft and satellites, but its purpose is still the same – to give reliable advance warning of the danger of drifting ice. Every year on the anniversary of the sinking of the *Titanic* the Ice Patrol places a wreath at latitude 41° 46'N, longitude 50° 14'W in the Atlantic Ocean as a memorial to those who died and as a tribute to those who aided the survivors. Although the discovery of the wreck in 1985 showed that the location was actually 41° 44'N, 49° 57'W.

For the White Star Line the loss of the *Titanic* was a major catastrophe and its sister ship, the *Olympic,* was withdrawn from service in order that its double bottom and bulkheads could be extended, and for additional lifeboats to be fitted. At the same time, the third sister, originally due to be named the *Gigantic,* was redesigned and eventually christened the *Britannic.*

All reports of the sinking emphasised that the loss of life would have been much greater if the Marconi wireless operators had not been on board the *Titanic.* This gave an immediate boost to the installation of radio in all ships. It also led to the ruling that there was to be a twenty-four-hour round-the-clock coverage and an emergency alarm system to waken a sleeping wireless operator. Never again would a ship be able to sit a few miles away and its captain claim that he did not know that another ship nearby was in danger. No, the people on the *Titanic* did not die in vain, but it is tragic that they had to die at all.

As mother could see no future for us in the New World, we had to make another sea voyage for our return journey to England. She booked us on a small ship called the *Celtic* which was due to sail on 25 April 1912 for Liverpool. This particular ship was chosen mainly because mother had made up her mind to be home well before her parents' Golden Wedding Anniversary on 15 July.

I was very surprised to see that she slept soundly every night on that return journey to England. 'What I dreaded has happened' she said to me, 'it's over and it can't happen again'.

I'm afraid that I was the one who was frightened on that second journey. I was absolutely hysterical with fright all the time we were on that ship. Even when we were back on dry land I had recurrent nightmares for years and suffered a great deal from the memories of that tragedy. I was terribly upset at the loss of my father, as was my mother. She was never quite the same again, mainly because she felt that the short period of pleasure in her life was all she was to have and it had now come to an end. I was also miserable because I could see my mother's unhappiness as she tried to start her life all over again without him.

We had no home of our own to go to when we arrived back in England so we had to stay with my mother's parents who were living in Chadwell Heath, about 3 miles from where we had lived in Seven

Kings. There was no question about returning to what had been our own home before emigrating. Not only had the house already been sold, but it would have been too large for just the two of us in any case.

However, we could not continue staying with relatives all the time so we had to find another home of our own. Fortunately, two doors away from my grandparents' house was a house which my father had built and had sold to a friend as an investment for the purpose of letting. The letting of houses now is much less common in Britain than it was many years ago because continuous rent control on private property for over seventy years made housing less suitable for investment purposes. But in 1912 it was common for people to buy houses in order to let them, and it was fortunate for us that this was so. This particular house became empty at just about the time we came back to England and the good lady who had originally purchased it from my father some years before said to my mother, 'I will be happy to sell it to you. You may have it and move into it as soon as you wish. But you do not need to pay me for it until you receive some money when your husband's will is settled and everything has been dealt with.'

So, because of her kindness, we were able to move into this house, which is still standing, in Whalebone Grove, Chadwell Heath. I lived there with my mother until she died in 1928 at the age of sixty-five, some sixteen years after the *Titanic* disaster.

Our standard of living dropped considerably compared with when my father had been alive. Although it was never necessary for mother to go out to work during those sixteen years, there were some very difficult times for us. Contrary to popular belief, we did not live in the lap of luxury as a result of the *Titanic* Disaster Fund which had been set up.

The relief fund had started with a collection carried out amongst the crew and passengers on the *Titanic*'s sister ship the *Olympic* as soon as news of the tragedy reached her. On the Tuesday after being picked up, the survivors on the *Carpathia* themselves set up a committee to collect donations for a general disaster fund. But the major appeal was that made by the Lord Mayor of London. It was a large-scale undertaking and collection boxes were even placed on the railings outside the Mansion House. The fund grew rapidly and almost developed into a mania with everybody and everything organising some scheme to raise money for the people who had suffered from the disaster. Because of the great loss of life, followed by a big public inquiry in New York and then an equally large inquiry in London, the tragedy was much more than the normal nine-day wonder. Many articles were written, excusing, criticising and blaming the designers, the builders, the shipping line and the British Board of Trade. Even the erudite magazine, *Scientific American,* published a number of articles and letters dealing with the structure of the *Titanic* and the inadequacy of the life-saving equipment. With all this continuous publicity the magnitude of the tragedy caught the sympathy of everybody and the final amount raised by the disaster fund – £414,066 including interest – still represents one of the largest sums of money ever raised in Great Britain following a tragedy. It was an enormous sum for 1912, equivalent to approximately £30 million at 2012 values.

For practical purposes, the administration of the fund was carried out by the Mansion House Committee in conjunction with several local subcommittees in the cities and towns such as Liverpool and Southampton in which survivors and dependants resided. After an initial distribution to survivors and dependants who were in financial distress, the remainder of the money (£383,754) was invested by the trustees in order to provide a regular income over an extended period. In this instance the trustees were the Lord Mayor of London and the Public Trustee. As the Public Trustee's office had only been established in 1906, this represented one of the biggest jobs which had arisen during its six years' existence, and remained a major responsibility until the fund was finally wound up in 1965.

Trustees of disaster funds are limited to some extent in the manner in which funds can be distributed and the Public Trustee operates a policy of aiming for a regular income for dependants, rather than distributing lump sums. This procedure was also carried out with the disaster funds for the *Empress of Ireland* (1914), the *Lusitania* (1915), and was similarly applied with the disaster funds of the later tragedies of HM Submarine *Affray* (1951) and the *Princess Victoria* (1953).

The Scheme of Administration of the *Titanic* Disaster Fund stated that it was 'for the aid and relief of widows, orphans and dependant relatives of the persons (whether crew or passengers) who lost their lives by reason of the foundering in the Atlantic Ocean on the 15 April 1912, of the steamship *Titanic*'. However, I have always felt that the fund was never applied in the manner the public had expected and survivors and dependants did not all benefit from it to the extent that they could have done. As with many disaster funds, the general public donate their money in a most generous manner but it then gets tied up with red tape, legal restrictions or restrictive covenants which prevent the money going to the people for whom it was contributed. There are, in fact, still large sums of money existing in Britain which were donated by the public with the intention of giving immediate relief to those in need but which have still not been used fully for the purposes for which they were intended. I am certain there is some need for a better arrangement to be made to deal with disaster appeals and the distribution of money raised in this way. The Public Trustee is not always or necessarily involved in dealing with a fund and it is not uncommon for fund administrators to get themselves so tied up with difficulties that the money accumulates in the banks instead of helping those in the manner contributors had probably intended.

It was not until nine months after the *Titanic* sank that my mother was told how much she would receive from the fund. Although she had been given $100 by the committee for immediate expenses. In line with a scale of payments laid down by the Mansion House Committee she was authorised to have one guinea (£1.05) per week for herself and three shillings and sixpence (17 ½ p) per week for me. Allowing for the increase in the cost of living over nearly eighty years, these sums would be worth about £76 and £13, respectively, at 2012 values. She also managed to persuade the fund administrators to pay a small amount to cover part of the cost of my education until I was eighteen, but that was all she had for me.

Some years later, after she had died, when all income from the Disaster Fund had ceased and I could only anticipate a very small income of my own, I wrote to the administrators asking if I could benefit from the fund in any way. It was, after all, because of the loss of my father that our standard of living had dropped and that my own future was financially insecure. But I was informed that as I 'had been aged under eighteen at the time of the disaster I had no right to anything in the fund as it was intended for dependants not survivors.' It did not seem to have occurred to the people responsible for setting up and running the fund that a person could be both a dependant and a survivor. I assume they felt that in helping to pay to have a child educated, presumably in order to earn a living, this exonerated the fund from any other responsibility.

At the end of 1957 more than £100,000 still remained invested for the fund, giving an income then of £3.50 per week to each of the seventy-nine dependants (but excluding dependants who were also survivors). A number of survivors, including myself, got together to try and have our cases reopened in the hope of receiving some benefit from the fund. Lawrence Beesley (the survivor who wrote the book *The Loss of the Titanic*) went to see the Public Trustee and was told that as the guidelines for administering the funds had been laid down by the government there was no way in which they could be varied for the benefit of the remaining survivors.

The fund was finally wound up completely in 1958 by purchasing annuities for the remaining dependants of the people who drowned. But the winding up was carried out without notifying any of the survivors and certainly no effort was made to provide people like me with annuities before it was closed, despite the considerable loss we had all suffered. It was only by later enquiries that I found out in 1965 that the fund no longer existed.

Unfortunately, my father could not have left very much money as he had had to sell his properties quickly in England in order to settle up with his creditors before starting up again in Canada. But what was available was at least sufficient to enable mother to buy the house and to see her through her remaining years.

Before the *Titanic* Disaster Fund started to assist with the cost of my education, I attended the small village school in Chadwell Heath. Later I was able to attend St Mary's Convent School in Western Road, Romford, although it meant a journey of several miles there in the morning and back in the evening. I stayed at that school until my basic education was complete at the age of sixteen. The education I received was of a very high standard and the discipline was firm. It was there that I was taught to take care with writing and speech and to be tidy. By modern standards it was a very formal education, but it did not appear to do us any harm and much of what I learnt was useful in later years.

Despite being what would now be called a deprived child in a one parent family, I did not grow up with an urge to smash windows or to bash old ladies over the head in order to steal handbags. My mother accepted her responsibilities towards me and did not seek to make feeble excuses by failing to keep the house clean, to provide meals or to keep me under control. Neither did I develop a multitude of psychological inhibitions, making it impossible for me to adjust to society. Whatever the faults that existed with our education in the early part of the twentieth century, it created fewer delinquents, layabouts and social outcasts than the present system appears to.

As I grew up, and during the whole of my adolescence, I tried to draw a complete curtain over my memory of the *Titanic* disaster. Because it was so painful and horrifying to me I had no wish to recall it unnecessarily. For many years I was too frightened of the sea and what I had seen it do to be able to talk about that fateful voyage. I think now it would have been better if I had not bottled it up so much for such a long time and if other people had talked freely about it in front of me. Instead I would get up and run out of the room if it came up in conversation. Because of this, it lay at the back of my mind for many years and probably affected me until I eventually made the necessary effort to overcome its influence upon me.

7

GROWING UP

Music has always played a major part in my life and I developed a great love for it when I was very young. Even at the age of seven my singing was very good, as my mother had pointed out in the letter she wrote on board the *Titanic.* She was, of course, well aware of my love for music and because she was concerned about how I might react after the disaster and the loss of my father, decided to encourage this interest. She bought me a piano as soon as she could possibly afford it and I spent a great deal of my time learning to play and losing myself in the totally absorbing world of self-created music. I progressed so well that I passed my various Associated Board examinations at quite an early age and shortly after I left school at sixteen, I started to teach music to young children. I did not aim to build up a large music school, but I found it gave me a great deal of pleasure to be able to pass on my love and knowledge of music to even a few who wished to learn. It was my first real experience of giving a service or guiding others and, looking back on it, it formed the basis of my later involvement in working with the public. I continued teaching music for a number of years and while doing this was encouraged further to develop my singing by a family friend, Claude Dyer, who was himself a successful baritone. Claude and his wife, Ida, had been married in Chadwell Heath two months after we returned from the USA and I can still remember my grandfather picking me up so that I could see the bride in her beautiful white dress and veil. Unfortunately, that cost us our dinner, as I had been carrying a trug of meat back from the butcher's and put it on the ground when I was picked up. When we had finished watching the bride and groom and went to pick up the trug we found that our steak and kidney had disappeared – inside our dog, Joe, who had followed us all the way.

We soon became friends with Claude and Ida Dyer and I greatly valued the help I received over the years from the whole Dyer family. Although I frequently reminded Claude that it was because of his marriage that I nearly started singing for my supper at a very early age. But he pointed out to my mother that I had a very good singing voice that he considered was worth training.

Mother had quite a job paying for the cost of the singing lessons; I was now over eighteen and the *Titanic* Disaster Fund administrators were not prepared to provide any additional assistance for my further training (or at any time during the remainder of my life). But somehow she scraped the money together to cover the expense and eventually, as a result of having a very good singing teacher, I was able to do quite a bit of professional singing as a soprano for many years. It opened a door for me to a completely new world and led to me meeting a large number of people who became my friends and later made their names in the entertainment world. In some cases I met them when their careers were just starting and before they had become household names. During the time I was having my voice trained, I continued giving music lessons, so that for several years the pattern of my life revolved around my love for music.

The area in which we lived during this time was a small village surrounded by farm land. Chadwell Heath derives its name from a well at a spring where St Chad was believed to have baptised his Saxon converts to Christianity, but the Parish church of St Chad was not actually consecrated until 1895. The small road in which mother had bought our new home was just off Whalebone Lane, which was a narrow tree-lined road leading past a few houses and cottages going northwards to Hainault Forest. The name had originated from two large whale jawbones which were hung over the iron gates at Whalebone House and were believed to have come from a whale washed ashore at Dagenham Breach in a great storm in 1658. Those jawbones remained there until shortly before the Second World War when they were removed to hang over the doors of Valence House. They are, however, still represented to this day in the sign of the Tollgate Public House which stands at the crossroads of Chadwell Heath High Road and Whalebone Lane.

In 1912, Chadwell Heath and Dagenham were part of the Romford Urban District in the county of Essex and the whole area was mainly open countryside and farm land, but I was to see a great change take place in the area over the next eighty years.

A number of the manor houses in the surrounding countryside had been vacated at the end of the nineteenth and the beginning of the twentieth centuries. One in particular was the Manor of Parsloes (the home of the Fanshaw family), which was empty but still standing for many years until it was eventually demolished in 1925. While I was young, trotting races used to be held in the grounds of the Manor. Parsloes Park in Dagenham now covers the land originally occupied by much of the estate.

Nearer to our home in Chadwell Heath was Wangey House. This had already lost part of its land and building to the Great Eastern Railway for the construction of Chadwell Heath railway station. The remainder of that house survived until just before the Second World War, but always looked a little out of place by the side of the railway line in a developing area.

But the manor house I have always loved most of all is Valence House. At that time it was occupied by a family called May whom my grandparents knew very well and I was often taken to visit them. It has always had an atmosphere of tranquillity, serenity and calm which I never cease to enjoy. Perhaps, because it still stands, I look upon the house as something secure and stable which has survived all the development and change which has taken place, almost like an oasis with which I have a special affinity. At one time it had a moat all the way round with a drawbridge. Part of that moat still remains around the house and comes alive each year when the swans arrive to build their nests in the shadow and peace of yester-year.

The First World War came upon us very soon after we settled into our new home in Chadwell Heath but, as there were no men in our small household, it did not impinge directly upon us, but the pain and suffering to families around us only served to remind us of our own loss and tragedy a short time before. The most outstanding memories I have of that war include seeing the Zeppelins passing overhead. Two of them were shot down very near to us, one coming down at Cuffley and the other at Billericay. They were majestic as they moved gracefully through the sky, but at the same time were a great menace to our safety.

Undoubtedly, the most unpleasant thing for us during the war was the news of the sinking of the *Lusitania* – a Cunard passenger liner carrying mainly US citizens. As it was little more than three years since the *Titanic* had sunk, the news of the torpedoing of the *Lusitania* on Friday 7 May 1915 took both Britain and America by storm. My mother was taking me to visit our relations at Rye and we were on Charing Cross railway station when the story broke in the newspapers. I think we both re-lived our own tragic experiences in a split second, thinking of the ship sinking and people screaming for help. All we could think about during our journey to Rye was those poor people and their families suffering as we had done; we knew how they felt. Altogether, 1,198 people died and only 761 were saved. On this occasion many of the lifeboats were unusable because of the severe listing of the decks as the ship sank. Despite this attack on a civilian ship carrying US citizens, it was another two years before the USA entered the First World War. Unfortunately, the sinking of the *Lusitania* revived our own troubled memories of the *Titanic* for some time afterwards.

Soon after the end of the First World war we all had another shock. We learnt that the London County Council was going to construct a huge housing estate to cover the whole area between Chadwell Heath and the River Thames 4 miles away. All the land around the farms and mansions so familiar to us was destined to be bricks and mortar instead of trees and fields. My mother found this further change difficult to accept because
from Chadwell Heath railway station we could see over the farms with their acres of cabbages as far as the river, and clearly visible to us were the red sails of the barges that moved up and down to the London docks. But over the next ten years a major part of the largest municipal housing estate in the world was constructed out in the flat Essex countryside.

It was some time before we fully appreciated the magnitude of the proposed development and the total change it would bring to the character of the area. Over 25,000 dwellings, mainly houses, were constructed between 1921 and 1934 and the population increased by 70,000 in just the five years prior to 1926. There were few facilities for the new tenants on the estate, although the homes were readily occupied by people who moved from the slums of the East End of London. Within the boundaries of the large estate there were no cinemas and few public houses, and transport to places outside the district was generally poor. Because of this, local people, like myself, who enjoyed singing or playing instruments used to give Saturday night concerts in the newly built schools. These were always well attended and continued for years as the estate expanded.

It was as a result of the growth of the Becontree Estate that the Dagellham Urban District was created covering most of the LCC estate and including Chadwell Heath. The first offices for the Council were in the beautiful Valence House, which ensured its preservation while development and expansion occurred in all directions.

The name Dagenham is derived from Daeccanham (meaning Daecca's village), an old Saxon settlement first mentioned towards the end of the seventh century. It is also listed as forming part of the Becontree Hundred in the twelfth century. Many of the old historic names associated with Becontree and Dagenham are still preserved in the street names on the estate. Reede Road, where Archbishop George Carey lived as a boy after the Second World War, is named after Roger Reede, a fifteenth-century landowner; and Alibon Road gets it name from Sir Richard Alibon who occupied the Manor of Dagenham in the seventeenth century, while Chitty's Lane has obtained its name from Sir Thomas Chitty who was Lord Mayor of London in 1750. The whole area is steeped in history submerged under the red-brick houses and grey pavements. Some of the history can be seen displayed in the museum still housed in Valence House.

When the construction of the Becontree Estate commenced I was well into my teens. Because of the traumatic experience we had shared my mother and I grew even closer together. As a result I became very adult in my outlook and attitude at an early age. She never gave me evasive answers to even the most embarrassing questions that I asked so that I did not have to unlearn the distortions and half-truths normally given to inquisitive children who enquired about 'not nice subjects'. This sometimes created problems at school, particularly when I told other children that babies were neither found under gooseberry bushes nor delivered by over-worked storks.

It was while I was still young that I started to take an interest in politics. This probably occurred because my mother was an intelligent, capable woman who did not hesitate to discuss the Country's and World's problems and events with me despite the difference in our years. She obviously believed that if I was old enough to know the marvels of the human body then I was old enough to be aware of man's inhumanity to man, and of the problems I might encounter later in life.

I have no time for people who generalise by saying that the young start off with left-wing views and move steadily to the right as they get older. As far as I can tell my basic political views have not greatly changed with age, maturity or experience. I became a firm

Conservative believing essentially in the freedom of the individual against the collectivism of the state. This is in no way incompatible with a deep and genuine concern for the less fortunate people in society. I have never been able to see the value in the Socialistic ideology of collectivism; this is probably because of a conversation I heard, when I was a teenager, between my mother and one of her friends. The friend was trying to explain the advantages of a Socialist economy and said, 'Socialism means we all work for the benefit of each other because we are the state. If you have a field of potatoes and I have a field of parsnips then you give me some of your potatoes and I give you some of my parsnips.' With disarming perception my mother put her finger on the fundamental weakness of the argument by replying, 'But I don't like parsnips!'

So a Conservative I was and a Conservative I have remained. Despite all the suffering I have seen and undergone, the industrial problems I was later to encounter and the very sincere Socialists with whom I have worked, I consider that Socialism and Communism are less able to provide for peoples' needs than is Conservatism. In claiming that all people are equal the idealists also treat them as if all people are identical in ability, intellect, aspirations and desires. One of the first lessons I learnt in this very real world was that everyone is an individual and deserves to be treated as one, with consideration for their weaknesses and encouragement for their abilities. I do not consider myself a deep thinking philosophical politician, but rather as a person who believes in encouraging enterprise and self-reliance and providing opportunity.

Because of my early political interest I helped form, and became secretary of, the Junior Imperial League (forerunner of the Young Conservative organisation) in the Romford Parliamentary Constituency. Our nickname was an obvious one, and I remember when we turned up in force at one public political meeting the chairman greeted our arrival by announcing from the platform, 'The Himps his wiv us.' *We certainly were, and* we *made our presence felt.*

We had a thriving political organisation and I used to walk for miles around the constituency attending committee meetings, meeting new members and canvassing in elections. During all this time I was doing my best to forget about the *Titanic* and the loss of my father. I didn't talk about it and I am sure that many of my friends had no idea of the traumas I had suffered as a little girl. As a result I had great fun, but it all had a serious purpose to it and involved a great deal of hard work. The experiences I gained stood me in great stead later in my life.

Until the Becontree Estate was built the Parliamentary constituency was essentially rural with the villages like Dagenham and Chadwell Heath and the focal point of the area, the market town of Romford, possessing the major populations. As the houses in the estate became occupied so the electorate increased and as a result the Romford constituency became the largest numerically in the United Kingdom. Redistribution into several smaller constituencies did not take place until 1945, after the Second World War. So that our General Election campaigns of 1922 and onwards, in which I participated as a very active 'Imp', were extremely demanding on the voluntary workers.

I remained involved in politics in Dagenham all the years that I was physically active and able to do a useful job.

With all the keenness of youth I tackled every type of political task that came my way, little thinking that years later I would become a constituency chairman, then the president and frequently be involved with the selection of Parliamentary candidates. I could always claim to have had plenty of first-hand experience at all the tasks I asked others to undertake.

The next major upheaval in my life occurred when my mother died in 1928 when she was sixty-five years old. There is, of course, nothing exceptional in being left an orphan when you are twenty-three, but that doesn't make it any easier to accept and I realised for the first time that, apart from music and singing, I had no other proper training or qualifications by which I could earn a living.

I had reached a stage at which I didn't know what to do. Now that my mother was dead I had no desire to continue living in the house she had purchased and my career prospects were vague to say the least. However, amongst the people to whom I wrote informing them of my mother's death was an uncle in Australia. He was my father's elder brother, his only relative other than the sister in New York. I had never met my uncle, but we had always kept up a very close correspondence with him and his wife even after the *Titanic* tragedy. In this instance, directly he heard that my mother had also died, he wrote back saying, 'Why don't you come and live with us in Australia? We've got a beautiful climate and would love to have you here in Perth.'

It was more than the prospect of a warm climate which attracted me to Australia. My uncle was also a fine musician and had a son who had inherited his musical ability. As my cousin was the conductor of the Rose Bay (Sydney) Orchestra in New

Above: 1. *Titanic*'s near miss with the SS *New York* shortly after departing from Southampton on her maiden voyage, noon Wednesday 10 April. The Hart family boarded *Titanic* at Southampton.

Below right: 2. The Hart Family; Benjamin, Eva (aged seven) and Esther, photographed before leaving for Canada.

Below left: 3. Eva aged five, two years before setting out on the fateful voyage.

Above: 4. The *Titanic* ablaze with lights heading out of Cherbourg harbour at 8.30 p.m. on Wednesday 10 April 1912.

Left: 5. Benjamin Hart, Eva's Father, photographed in the car he owned shortly before the family sailed aboard the *Titanic*.

Below left: 6. Forward first class grand stairway immortalised in the *Titanic* film. The top landing led out directly onto the boat deck.

This page: 7, 8, 9 & 10. Interior photographs of some of the first class areas aboard *Titanic*. Clockwise from left, first class the reading room, the Café Parisien, the gym and reception room.

FIRST CLASS STATE ROOMS

POST MAIL ROOM

THE BUCKLED PLATES

BILGE KEEL

DOUBLE BOTTOM

KEEL

ICE PENETRATING THE DOUBLE BOTTOM

Opposite: 11. Contemporary cross-section illustration of the *Titanic* showing where it was thought the iceberg struck.
Above: 12. View of the forecastle of *Titanic*, showing the crow's nest.
Below: 13. Photograph of *Titanic*'s sister ship, *Olympic*, in 1911.

Above: 14. Rear starboard boat deck and the second class promenade area. This is an area Eva and her father would have explored on their tour of the ship on the first few days of the voyage. The lifeboats shown are 15 (nearest), 13, 11 and 9. In the distance can just be seen lifeboats 7, 5 and 3.

Left: 15. A view of the port side of *Titanic*, the area of the Hart family's cabin. It also shows the rear port side boat deck where Eva and her mother escaped in lifeboat 14 (from left to right the lifeboat numbers are 10, 12, 14 and 16).

This page: 16, 17 & 18. Views of some of the deck areas of the *Titanic*. Clockwise from top, promenade deck (A) which ran nearly the whole length of the ship. Many female passengers were loaded into lifeboats from this deck. Forward starboard boat deck, the lifeboats shown are 3 (nearest), 5 and 7. Port side towards the stern of the ship showing position of lifeboat 16.

Above spread: 19. Cutaway drawing of *Titanic* reproduced in newspapers in late April 1912 showing the suspected section (heavy black line) 'torn out' by the collision with the iceberg. Since the discovery of the wreck, scientists have used sonar to examine the area and discovered the iceberg had caused the hull to buckle, allowing water to enter *Titanic* between her steel plates. The illustration also shows much of the layout of the ship.

Opposite page centre: 20. After deck of *Titanic*'s sister ship, *Olympic* 1911, looking towards the stern. Another deck-area Eva and her father would have explored.

Opposite page, bottom left & right: 21 & 22. Mrs Esther Hart's letter to her mother written from the *Titanic*.

Below: 23. A 1912 drawing of *Titanic*'s collision with the iceberg, reproduced in an American newspaper following the disaster.

Marconi Wires

1st Point of Contact with Ice

Submerged shelf of Iceberg

Chart House

Bridge

4 Forward Boats

Boat Deck

4 Stern Boats

Starboard side

Direction of Iceberg after Contact

Submerged shelf of Iceberg

Submerged Bulk of Iceberg

STRIKES STARBOARD BOW ·12 ft AFT

11 45 P.M.

Above: 24. Another 1912 illustration of *Titanic* striking the iceberg, which also gives a birds-eye view of her upper decks.

Left: 25. '11.45 p.m. *Titanic* strikes an iceberg with its starboard bow, 12 feet aft.' This is the first in a series of six sketches executed on board *Carpathia* by Lewis Skidmore (a young art teacher) based on conversations with survivor Jack Thayer following the rescue. The timings listed in this series of illustrations have since 1912 been revised somewhat.

Opposite: 26. A cutaway illustration of the *Titanic* as it scraped along the side of the iceberg. A French *Titanic* survivor described the moment: 'Through the portholes we saw the ice rubbing against the ship's side'.

First Class | Lounge | Promenade

Private Suite | Promenade

orridor

ath Rooms

ICEBERG
From 50 to 100 feet
according to various
accounts

st Class | Dining | Saloon

Companion way Stairs | Second Class

← Starboard port holes

t Class Dining Saloo

Water Line

Boiler Room

SETTLES BY HEAD · BOATS ORDERED OUT   12.05 A.M

SETTLES TO FORWARD STACK
BREAKS BETWEEN STACKS   ~1.40 A.M.

Top left: 27. '12.05 a.m. *Titanic* settles by head, boats ordered out.'
Top right: 28. Wallace Hartley, leader of *Titanic*'s band that Eva remembers hearing playing on t[...]
boat deck before she escaped on lifeboat 14.
Centre left: 29. '1.40 a.m. *Titanic* settles to forward stack, breaks between stacks'.
Centre right: 30. Captain of the *Titanic*, Edward J. Smith.
Above left: 31. Lawrence Beesley, fellow survivor of the disaster. Eva met Beesley in 1958 at a reuni[...]
of *Titanic* survivors following the London premiere of the film-version of Walter Lord's account [...]
the sinking, *A Night To Remember*.
Above right: 32. Charles Lightoller, Second Officer of the *Titanic* and the officer with over[...]
responsible for loading the lifeboats on the port side of the ship where Eva and her mother escape[...]
Eva only recalls being assisted by Fifth Officer Lowe.

Above left: 33. John Jacob Astor. The seven-year-old Eva was unaware of the large number of distinguished passengers aboard *Titanic*.
Above right: 34. Guglielmo Marconi whose wireless operators helped save Eva's life.
Below: 35. A typical wireless room of an ocean liner of the period.

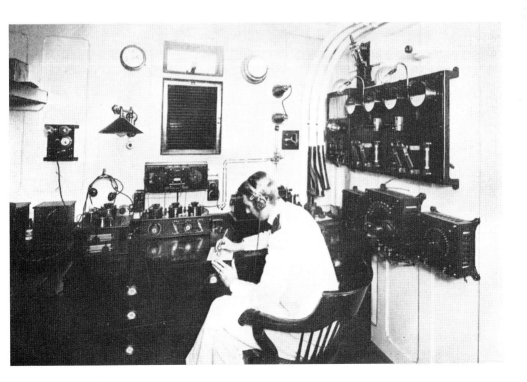

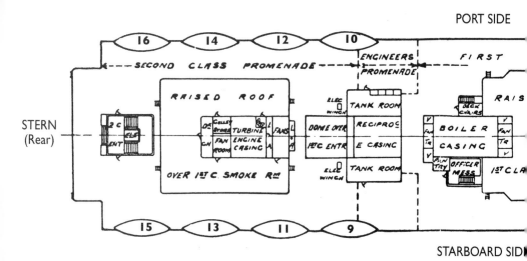

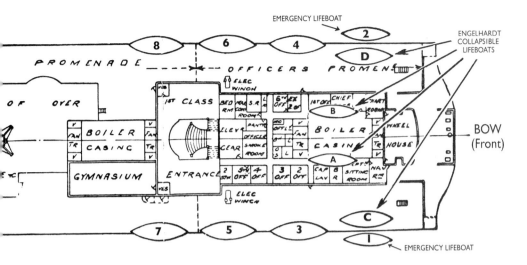

Above spread: 36. Plan of the boat deck of the *Titanic* showing the position of all 20 lifeboats 1 to 16 and collapsible A, B, C & D.

Opposite: 37. A 1912 illustration of the farewells between wives and husbands. Eva recalls what her father's last words to her were: 'Stay with your mummy and hold her hand tightly like a good girl'. It also shows how women and children were being loaded into the lifeboats from the promenade deck A rather than from the boat deck. The scared child to the left of the image clutching her mother could easily be Eva.

Right: 38. A 1912 illustration showing the loading of lifeboats from the forward port boat deck.

"A" DECK
70 feet above
the water

"B" DECK
from which many
of the women were
taken into the boats

"The Titanic looked enormous"

Boat Deck clear of boats

"The bows & bridge completely under water"

"Sea calm as a pond There was just a gentle heave"

"The starlight night was beautiful"

Stern
2nd class
Section of ship

"Every porthole
& saloon was
blazing with light"

42. Survivors look on in horror as *Titanic* sinks.

FORWARD END FLOATS,
THEN SINKS

1.50 A.M

Above & opposite page, top: 43 & 44. Eva on the final moments of *Titanic*: 'Slowly, very slowly, we could see the *Titanic* getting lower in the water. As the slope of the decks became even greater there was an increasing amount of noise, from the people still on board, from loose articles sliding along the decks. Then, for a short time, she seemed to hang almost vertically as if suspended from the sky with her stem clearly above the water.' Eva, along with a smallish group of survivors, believed that *Titanic* broke in two as she sank. She was finally proven correct when the wreck was discovered in two distinct parts by Bob Ballard's expedition in 1985.

Page 16 & 17 image: 39 & 40. These two contemporary images show the lowering of the lifeboats during the early stages of the disaster. *Titanic* is not yet low in the water and the lifeboats had to travel 70 feet from the boat deck to the sea.

Last page spread: 41. By the time Eva and her mother escaped from *Titanic* (about 1.25 a.m.) the ship's position was more like that shown in this spread. This image shows the rear port boat deck being clear of lifeboats (which it was by around 1.50 a.m.) so the situation wasn't quite as desperate as shown here. Eva's lifeboat was launched from this side and from the area marked with an arrow, 'Boat Deck clear of boats'.

STERN SECTION:
PIVETS AMIDSHIPS AND
SWINGS OVER SPOT WHERE FORWARD SECTION SANK

2.00 A.M

Right: 45. *41° 16'N; 50° 14'W* by Norman Wilkinson. This painting was commissioned as a frontispiece by the publisher of Filson Young's 1912 account of the sinking, *Titanic*, published in London just 37 days after the disaster. Over the years it has been much criticised for apparent inaccuracies but when Eva was shown the image she said 'That's exactly how it was'.

Funnel for auxiliary Machinery & ventilation

SPACE OCCUPIED BY RECIPROCATING & TURBINE ENGINES

WATER LINE

3 Forward Funnels carrying off Products of combustion from Main Boilers

SPACE OCCUPIED BY BOILERS

Opposite: 46. This 1912 illustration shows the more conventionally-held view that *Titanic* sank in one piece.

Above: 47. 'Final position in which *Titanic* stayed for several minutes before the final plunge', the final sixth sketch executed on board *Carpathia* by Lewis Skidmore based on conversations with survivor Jack Thayer.

48. View from *Carpathia* of the iceberg which sank the *Titanic*. Captain Rostron of the *Carpathia*: 'It was a beautiful morning, a clear sun burning on sea and glistening on the icebergs. On every side there were dozens of these monsters so wonderful to look at, so dreadful to touch.'

49. *Titanic* survivors approaching *Carpathia*. Eva's lifeboat (number 14) was heavily laden, unlike many others. Eva and her mother were transferred mid-ocean to free up space in a lifeboat to venture back to attempt save survivors stranded in the freezing Atlantic waters. Eva was separated from her mother during this process and the two weren't reunited until they were both aboard *Carpathia*.

Above: 50. The *Carpathia*. Eva: 'Our boat must have been one of the last to be cleared as it was about 8.30 a.m. before I was actually on board the ship. We were almost hysterical with fright at this new terror of having to get from the surface of the ocean back up the side of a ship. We were each put into a large canvas bag with our heads poking out at the top, and several 'bags' were then put into a lifting net which was winched up very quickly by a wheel on the deck. And so we arrived wet, cold and frightened. I was more frightened by this experience than by almost anything else that happened in the whole of those tragic events.'

Right: 51. Captain Arthur Rostron, of the *Carpathia*, the ship that picked up Eva, her mother and the other survivors from the *Titanic*.

52. *Titanic* survivors on the deck of *Carpathia*. Eva: 'While I was still crying for my mother, between dozing and being comforted by strangers, she was going from one part of the ship to another asking everyone she could if they had seen me. It was much later in the day before she discovered me, still miserable and huddled under borrowed clothing.'

53. The *Titanic*'s 13 surviving lifeboats in New York. Their nameplates and White Star flags were removed and the lifeboats disappeared.

Above: 54. Interior of the Cunard Line pier all cleared out ready to receive the survivors of the *Titanic* on arrival of the *Carpathia*, where they were met by relatives, doctors and nurses.

Right: 55. How the news of the disaster reached Londoners.

Above: 56. Eva and her mother Esther (right) on their return to England. They sailed on the *Celtic* from New York on 25 April 1912. Eva proudly hold aloft her new doll, bought for her by her mother to replace the teddy bear she left aboard *Titanic*.

Left: 57. Eva on the quayside in New York after the disaster.

58. Eva in 1912 after returning to England.

59. Esther Hart, Eva's mother in 1922.

Left: 60. Eva as a school girl.

Below: 61. Eva with her French Bulldog *c.*1960. Eva had eagerly sought out the French bulldog owned by Robert W. Daniel on board *Titanic* and her father had promised to buy her one once they reached Canada.

Right: 62. Eva with Bertram Dean another survivor, signing pictures of the *Titanic*. Bertram was a third class passenger aged only one when the *Titanic* sank and escaped in lifeboat 10.

Below: 63. Eva (right) in 1991 with fellow *Titanic* survivor Ruth Blanchard nee Becker. She was 12 at the time of the sinking, was travelling second class and saved in lifeboat 13.

Above: 64. Eva with fellow survivors from the *Titanic* disaster at the dedication of the new memorial to the musicians who went down with the *Titanic* after playing to the very end. Left to right, Edith Haisman, neé Brown (second class passenger aged fourteen when the *Titanic* sank and saved in lifeboat 14), Millvina Dean (third class passenger aged only two months when the *Titanic* sank and escaped in lifeboat 10), Bertram Dean (Millvina's brother) and Eva.

Below 65. Eva (right) with fellow survivor Edith Haisman at the unveiling of the *Titanic* memorial at the National Maritime Museum, Greenwich 15 April 1995.

South Wales, I knew I would be in good company and probably have the opportunity to continue with my singing. So, with some trepidation, I started making the arrangements for the sea trip to the other side of the world. I was far from happy about the prospect of such a long sea journey, but that was 1928 and it was not then possible to fly from England to Australia. So, if I wanted to go, there was only one way to do it and I had to overcome my phobias as best I could.

While making these preparations I also wrote to my mother's godson who lived in Singapore. He was fourteen years older than me. Mother and he had been devoted to each other and I had grown very fond of him. As I had no brothers or sisters I always looked upon him as an elder brother. So at this time in my letter I told him of my plans now that mother had died. He immediately sent me a cable telling me not to go straight to Australia but to visit him in Singapore first of all.

This still meant that I had to travel on a ship, but I forced myself to go by concentrating on the great pleasures and possibilities before me. Despite this attempt at a positive attitude, it still meant that I suffered agonies all the time I was preparing for the journey. I thought I would die of fright when I went on board that ship. For two days and nights I stuck in my cabin completely terrified and feeling very seasick. Gradually, however, I realised that the ship was still afloat and I was still alive. I also realised that nothing I could do was likely to determine whether or not we reached the intended destination. To a certain extent I managed to overcome my fears and I think it did me a lot of good in starting to work the subconscious aspects of the *Titanic* out of my system.

The voyage to Singapore which took me through the Mediterranean and the Suez Canal was very smooth until we entered the Indian Ocean on our way to Bombay and Colombo. It was at this point we met the monsoons. Incredible as it may seem, despite the fact that the ship was pitching and tossing I was not in the least afraid. Some of the other passengers seemed much more frightened. My fear of the sea only returned when the weather was calm again – I obviously still associated disasters at sea with the cold, calm weather we had when the *Titanic* sank. It was quite a relief when we eventually reached the beautiful island of Singapore and I felt rather pleased with myself for having managed to last the journey.

My 'elder brother', Fred, met me when the ship docked and drove me to his lovely home. He held a senior executive position with the Firestone Rubber Company and had a company house in Tanglin, the best residential area of the island. He and his wife, Winnie, who had no children of their own, made a great fuss of me during my stay. I used the time to get out and about as much as possible and found Singapore a gracious place. It was very difficult to imagine that a hundred years earlier it had been mainly swampland. I stayed in Singapore with Fred and Winnie for several weeks and also saw a great deal of the beautiful states which now form Malaysia, before continuing my sea voyage to Australia. I was fortunate enough to be driven, in a large, comfortable Studebaker, all over the Malayan peninsular during my stay. I could well understand why the British managers and planters found it all so enchanting. The Malays were most delightful, warm and kind people, and the whole journey, which included a trip across to what was then French Indo-China, Siam and Cambodia, was quite incredible and immensely enjoyable. For a short time I lived in a completely different world, totally captivated by the splendour of buildings like the famous temple of Angkor Watt. I was completely intoxicated and overwhelmed by the sheer wonder of all these marvelous places, by the hot steamy jungle, by the variety of flowers and birds, the colour of the butterflies, and the houses in the native villages. It was all so new to me and so different, helping greatly to distract me from my memories of the past and my worries and apprehensions of the future.

I was not able to visit that part of the world again for forty-seven years, until 1976, when I was on my way home after another visit to Australia. This time I travelled by airplane. During that time, Singapore had been totally transformed, but the bustle and atmosphere of the older parts of Singapore remained. I was quite surprised to find that the house in which I stayed with Fred and Winnie was still there, but was due to be demolished to make way for more tall blocks of apartments to accommodate Singapore's growing population.

Despite the pleasures of Singapore and Malaya and the kindness with which I had been received I was determined to continue my journey to the rest of my family in Perth. Getting to Australia from Singapore in 1929 was quite difficult and very different from now. But I had spent twelve weeks in Singapore and Malaya, taking the opportunity to relax and trying to get over the loss of my mother and the reality of being an orphan and I felt I had to make the effort to continue to Australia where there could be the real possibility of building a proper career. But I could not find an ordinary passenger ship to go direct from Singapore down to Western Australia, my intended destination, as the only normal passenger route was by the Dutch Line down the east coast of the country to Sydney.

In 1929, Western Australia was still a fairly inaccessible spot and poorly developed. But by this time I felt I had become a seasoned traveller, although I had not overcome my fear of the sea and of ships. So I decided to go to Fremantle by the only direct route cattle boat. I have no doubt that some of my lesser friends will consider that this was an appropriate way for me to travel! The cattle boat was in total contrast to what I had experienced many years before on the *Titanic.* It had room for only seven passengers in rather limited accommodation and there was not a great deal of space for us to walk around the ship. The prime responsibility of the shipping line was the care of all the magnificent cattle which were being taken to various animal breeding farms to improve the stock. Although taking second place to the more important cattle, the seven passengers were also treated very well. Being a cattle boat for use in hot climates meant that the animals were kept in open holds. As a result, there was only limited space for us to stroll around and most of our exercise was restricted to the fly walks around the holds. From our point of view it was fortunate that the trip progressed by a series of short hauls from one small port to another. The frequent stops certainly added greatly to the pleasure of the journey and I had a most enjoyable time.

As a result, the complete cruise extended for several weeks. From Singapore we went first to Java, then to Sumatra, Banka and Bali before reaching Darwin in northern Australia. Then in lovely warm weather we sailed down the west coast stopping to unload cattle at small ports like Derby, Broome, Port Headland, Roebourne, Carnarvon and Geraldton, before reaching Fremantle. I consider myself fortunate to have had the opportunity to visit remote places that even most Australians have never seen. We stayed several days in each port while unloading and loading were carried out and during this time I was able to explore the small towns and see local activities like the pearl fishing at Broome. It was all very fascinating and a marvellous experience; I was very pleased I had decided to travel in this way. Although the trauma from the memory of the *Titanic* remained with me. I certainly gained some idea of the magnitude of Australia and I think that I was able to get some impression of the great potential of that country that still exists there even now.

There was a great advantage in that long, slow, lazy voyage as it gave me a chance to think about my future as well as to get to know my fellow passengers. These included the then well-known author-traveller J. H. Curie, whose books about remote parts of the world enthralled readers during the 1930s.

He was a most interesting person with whom to converse as he could talk knowledgeably about most subjects. When I later read the incredible books he had written about his journeys to many countries I found he wrote as he spoke. In his books he opened up the whole world to the reader, even anticipating events such as over-population and racial problems. I have often regretted that I did not spend more time in his company, although the journey was interesting and full enough in any case.

Eventually the long, slow, lazy journey had to come to an end and the cattle boat tied up at its final destination, Fremantle. There I was met by my uncle, Joshua Hart, and his wife, Maud, who took me to their home in Perth. They were well established in the local community where uncle Joshua was the local schools' inspector. He was also acknowledged to be a superb musician and was in constant demand to play the violin at concerts in Western Australia. Through him and my cousin Lionel in Sydney I was able to do a lot of singing.

That part of Australia has marvellous weather, a Mediterranean type climate, so that citrus fruits can be grown without any effort, palm trees abound and snow is virtually unknown. It is absolutely glorious. I had arrived in time for Christmas 1929, although the marvellous weather made it difficult for me to realise that it was December and that back home in England it would be cold, frosty and even snowy. That year I had my first ever experience of eating a traditional Christmas dinner of turkey, pudding and mince pies in blazing sunshine at 38°C (100°F) on the beach. It really was a Christmas with a difference. It was so hot that despite the tempting appearance of the blue sea we didn't dare bathe until the sun had started setting. So we enjoyed our meal under huge sunshades near the water's edge.

I stayed in Perth until after the Christmas festivities were over and then took off again to visit the eastern side of that enormous country. By this time I felt I had some control over my fears of the sea and as I only had the choice between four or five days on a train tearing through desert landscapes or another sea voyage, I chose the latter. This time the journey was on a small ship sailing from Fremantle to Sydney. I certainly preferred the greater freedom of movement on the ship, and the journey, which took about a week, included short stops at Adelaide and Melbourne. As a result, I was able to take additional opportunities for sightseeing. When the ship sailed into Sydney's great natural harbour the great Sydney Harbour Bridge was still under construction. It looked very odd with the two parts of the arch being built out across the bay to meet each other. The final key piece to the bridge was fitted later during my stay in New South Wales on 19 August 1930, though the bridge was not finally completed and officially opened for traffic for another two years. Even now, after more than sixty years, it is still the largest steel arch bridge in the world and bestrides the harbour like the Colossus of Rhodes, but is more affectionately known as the 'old coat hanger'.

I had great expectations of Sydney and New South Wales as I hoped to be able to do a great deal of singing. My cousin, Lionel, and his wife, had a flat in an apartment block near the now famous Bondi Beach. In his role as the conductor of the Rose Bay Orchestra a great deal of his work was concerned with entertaining cinema audiences watching silent films. Although, whilst I was there the 'talkies' took over at the cinemas and most of the musicians were no longer required. Fortunately, from my point of view, broadcasting was developing very rapidly and I was able to earn some money singing over that relatively new medium.

Once again, I took advantage of the opportunity to do a great deal of sightseeing in and around the south-eastern part of Australia, including Canberra, which was at that time being rapidly constructed with its regular pattern of roads and government buildings. Around me I saw a nation undergoing the difficulties of growing up and finding its feet; with bush being turned into towns, roads being laid where kangaroos ran wild, rivers being harnessed for their power, and above all, the raw and slightly brash enthusiasm of a people who knew they had a sound future ahead and a nation ready to build.

In spite of the fact that they have all been constructed over the same period of time, the cities in Australia each possess their own character and quality. I have always found Melbourne to be the most English of cities, but the rapid changes in weather are most disconcerting and as bad as anything in Great Britain. I experienced almost every type of weather including enormous temperature changes all in a matter of hours, so that one minute you need a fur coat and the next a bikini. It was a bit too unpredictable for my liking.

I found Tasmania to be the part of Australia with a landscape most like England, and it is particularly reminiscent of parts of Devon. Just visiting it made me feel very homesick. As it is a bit further south and an island, its climate is cooler than that of mainland Australia. The fruit grown there is amongst the best in the world and nothing can beat a fresh, homegrown Tasmanian apple. The island's natural harbour at Hobart is second only to that of Sydney for quality and splendour.

Before returning to Western Australia I also made a longer visit to Adelaide. I had been impressed by the fact that it was a nice, quiet city, well justifying its title of 'The City of Churches'. It was the centre of the then developing Australian wine industry. For the first time in my life I saw acres of vineyards, the vines heavy with grapes of various colours just waiting to be picked. Whenever I see a bottle of Australian sherry or wine I think of that short time I spent enjoying the pleasure of Adelaide.

I had originally thought that I might stay in Australia permanently, or at least for a long time. But after a great deal of sightseeing all over that vast country, as well as meeting many different people through my singing, I realised that I was still unsettled. Because of this I decided it was time to return to Perth and think about my future a bit more. By this time, travelling itself did not worry me at all and once again I undertook the sea voyage back to Fremantle. Even though I still did not like to talk or think about the *Titanic* and the tragedy, I had at least faced up to one part of the shadow that had been cast over my life.

Back in Perth I tried to occupy myself with singing once again. Broadcasting was expanding quite rapidly and I was engaged for several performances on the radio. I enjoyed these immensely and was well received by the listening audience. But I still could not settle down. After a short time I came firmly to the conclusion that despite the lovely weather, the countryside and the very caring family in Perth, Australia wasn't for me as a permanent home.

I was well aware by this time that I needed to put down some permanent roots somewhere and to find a regular source of income. Although I could talk about some of my problems with my relations I still missed the close relationship I had enjoyed with my mother and would certainly have benefited by some guidance from my father if only he had been alive. Looking back on that very enjoyable era in Australia, I think I may have left England too soon after my mother's death. Although it may also have been that I was in

Australia at a time when it was undergoing a rapid transition and it felt almost as if nothing had any permanence.

Whatever it was, I was feeling upset within myself and knew that I wanted to return to England where I thought there might be a chance of coming to terms with myself. So I said goodbye to my very kind relations and headed back for England. Only this time I travelled in more comfort on a scheduled passenger liner with fewer qualms and worries at all about the sea. Little did I think that it would be another forty-five years before I would return to visit Australia again and when I did I would be prepared to talk freely and openly about my childhood experiences on the *Titanic* when interviewed on radio and television.

8

IN BETWEEN

My initial problem, on my return to England in 1931 after my first Australian visit, was to find somewhere to live. I had no home of my own to return to as I had fully expected to stay permanently on the other side of the world. Fortunately, I was able to stay for a short time with a cousin living in Ilford while I started looking for a permanent job.

I did not feel that I could continue to rely solely on the money I could make from singing as it was rather irregular and unpredictable; particularly as the country was in the middle of an industrial depression with many people unemployed. So I decided that I needed to obtain a full-time job and to undertake any singing engagements only in the evenings and at weekends. Eventually I managed to secure a position in charge of the wholesale department of an expanding motor car dealers in Goodmayes, only a short distance from Chadwell Heath. This was a very responsible position for a woman to have in those days, and I was entering the business at a time when the growth of motoring was really beginning to take hold. It was also the first time I had really come into close contact with manual and semi-skilled workers in any numbers and many of the things I learnt there played a part in the welfare and public work I was later to undertake.

Amongst the people who were glad to see me back from my travels were Claude and Ida Dyer. Claude was a local business man as well as being a brilliant singer. He was a person of outstanding ability and played a major role in the local community in Chadwell Heath. While I had been in Australia enjoying myself, Claude had been elected to the Dagenham Urban District Council as a Ratepayer Association representative from Chadwell Heath and he remained on the Council for nine years during the period when the Becontree Estate was still growing and the local population increasing. It eventually covered most of Dagenham, a large part of Barking and part of Goodmayes.

Apart from the political changes in the area, the building of the Estate created many problems, not least for the very people it had been intended to benefit. Construction work continued for many years and it was difficult for a stable community to become established; this was certainly aggravated by lack of local entertainment and leisure facilities. The very ambitious development had not been completed even by 1939 when the Second World War came.

During the early period of the development many of the new residents had great problems because of lack of jobs or because they were financially worse off than they had been when living in London as they also had to pay train fares back to London each day for work. Eventually the situation was eased when the Ford Motor Company decided to locate a factory in the southern part of the area because of the available labour. Even so, a very large proportion of the Ford workers have always lived outside of Dagenham and the Becontree Estate.

The coming of Ford's by the side of the River Thames at Dagenham Breach led to further changes in the environment of the area I had loved so much when I was young. It used to be a place for Sunday walks by the River Thames, with beautiful tall bullrushes and attractive flowers. For bird-watchers it was a favourite spot, with a wide variety of species arriving at different times of the years. All along the river it was possible to watch the ships and barges passing slowly and gracefully to and from the London docks. But over a period of seven or eight years all that changed completely. It is difficult to visualise all that now when it has been replaced with large factory buildings, blocks of offices and rows of motor cars.

As a result of earning my own living, and being independently minded, I rented a small flat of my own in Chadwell Heath, and have lived there ever since. For a while life went along smoothly, with my time devoted to becoming familiar with the expanding motor trade during the daytime and singing during my free time. I became an inveterate theatre goer and tried to see most of the new plays as soon as they were produced in London.

Having overcome my fear of the sea, I spent most holidays on board ships in order to travel as widely as possible. I travelled all around the Mediterranean, visiting places like Marseilles, Malta and Genoa. For an unattached person like myself it was very reasonable as a first class ticket on a P & O liner for a Mediterranean cruise was then only £22. Work and play kept my time very fully occupied. During that period, for about ten years after my mother died, I had virtually pushed the *Titanic* disaster out of my mind. At the same time I started to lay the foundations of my long term future involvement in public and voluntary work as I appreciated that other people going through difficult periods of their lives also required help and encouragement.

I found my work extremely varied and as a result met a number of very interesting people. One of our regular visitors at the car dealers was a young man named Jack Waters. He came to the offices frequently as a representative for a wholesale car distributors. I came to know Jack very well as his father was a friend of Claude Dyer, and we also used to see him at cabaret parties and ladies' nights. Jack Waters went on to become famous under his professional name of Jack Warner, of *The Blue Lamp* fame, and eventually finished up as the star of the long running television series *Dixon of Dock Green* in the 1960s. The Waters family was a very talented one. Jack's two sisters, Elsie and Doris, also made their names, as *Gert and Daisy* and I was very pleased to participate in a radio show with them some years later.

It was during this time that Dagenham ceased to be an Urban District and received its Borough Charter on 1 October 1938. My copy of the Charter Record has photographs of the Becontree Estate and the, then, new Dagenham Civic Centre, which Claude Dyer had helped to plan. Unfortunately it only took twenty years for the councillors of the Borough to forget the wise words written by George Lansbury MP, Leader of the Labour Party, at the time of the granting of the Charter. He said:

There are many thousands of my friends living in the new townships and boroughs of Essex. They have come from overcrowded streets and tenements hoping to find health, recreation and rest along the countryside. I devoutly hope that as the days pass there will be an ever increasing determination to preserve and develop all the cultural, health and other social services. And that this part of Essex will preserve the cottage homes of England and never permit the erection of Block dwellings.

The Dagenham Civic Centre was originally in a very attractive setting, surrounded almost entirely by open land. In the 1970s it was overwhelmed by the very block buildings that George Lansbury abhorred, and the environment of Dagenham is that much poorer and congested for it.

At that time, despite the rumblings from Europe, few of us were aware of how all our lives were to be totally changed in the near future. What I thought was a period of calmness, with a smooth continuity of working, music and politics, was abruptly upset when war was declared in September 1939.

I have always found that life has a few tricks up its sleeve. My prelude to that War arose during my summer vacation in 1939 and became another memorable event that I am unlikely to forget. For my journey that year I left England on a lovely new liner, the *Pretoria Castle,* bound for the Canary Islands accompanied by my singing teacher. Shortly after our journey started, we learnt that Franco's government, having won the civil war in Spain, was being officially recognised by the British Government. Somehow, this affected the political control in Tenerife because, as soon as we landed, our passports were confiscated and we were taken away to the local police station where we were locked in the cells.

That was my first experience of any form of imprisonment, and not one that I ever wish to repeat. It was several hours before the local agent for the Union Castle Line managed to obtain our release. He explained to us that the political changes whilst we were en route meant we now needed a visa in order to land in the Canary Islands, so we had apparently offended the new government by breaking its freshly imposed regulations.

It was a great relief to get out into the fresh air again, away from the claustrophobic atmosphere of the cells. For the first time I had become aware of what it was like to lose one's liberty. Something I always bore in mind later in life when I became a magistrate.

Following that experience we left Tenerife as soon as possible and that very night caught a ferry to Las Palmas. This boat was absolutely filthy. It had not been cleaned after being used to transport Spanish soldiers during the civil war and was running alive with enormous cockroaches as well as lice and fleas. Nobody dared to try to sleep during the journey for fear of waking to find the cockroaches walking over them. To add to the misery many people were seasick due to a storm that blew up during the crossing.

Despite our expectations, on reaching Las Palmas our passports were confiscated again. It seemed that Franco was still suspicious of the British Government's intentions, and of us, because of his close friendship with Hitler and Mussolini. And, instead of the carefree holiday we had expected with sunbathing, swimming and sightseeing, we were confined to our hotel until we were due to leave. I never was clear what damage a group of British holidaymakers might cause the Fascist Government, or what military secrets we were likely to pick up from the islanders. But Franco did a great job in ruining my last real holiday before the Second World War.

There was no opportunity to do any travelling around the world during wartime although my singing was to take me to many obscure parts of England over the next few years. As I lived in an area that was an eastern suburb of London, I was well aware that Chadwell Heath was likely to suffer from any German bombing that occurred. Not only was the very busy Ford Motor Company only three miles away, but there were other major engineering and chemical companies in the area and we were only six miles as the crow (or bomber) flies from the Royal Group of Docks (now redeveloped as the incredible Docklands commercial centre in East London). So the whole of the area in which I lived and worked became a prime target for the bombers seeking to destroy British industry.

Before the air-raids started I had offered my services to the ARP and was told that in the event of war coming I would be valuable on communications. That sounded very important and I imagined myself coordinating the movement of transport, information and messages throughout the area. When war was declared I was hastily summoned to the bowels of the Civic Centre in Dagenham where I found I was in charge of all the telephone communications with the various ARP (Air Raid Precautions) posts which were dotted around the district. Because we were at the centre of the spider's web of communication we were very well protected. In this case it meant being about fifteen feet below ground, with no windows and inadequate ventilation. I found the conditions claustrophobic and often thought it was probably better in the small local concrete cube ARP posts which had been placed on street corners. They at least had direct access to the outside world and the wardens were able to get out to become part of the community and involved with the people; while I was cooped up taking telephone messages from one disembodied person to another and trying to prevent myself from becoming neurotic at the same time. How I survived as long as I did I don't know, but after a few weeks I really had had enough. I almost shouted with relief when I was told that the Borough Treasurer wanted to see me because he had a different job for me to do.

I was informed by the Borough Treasurer that he was going to be the official food officer for the district. Within the borough he was to organise and co-ordinate the food rationing that the Ministry of Food had decided to introduce throughout the country. He was looking for staff to set up the food offices and to deal with the issuing of the ration books to the 100,000 people for whom he was responsible. I must admit that I didn't require much persuasion to escape from my underground torture chamber and was ready to try almost any other job to help the war effort. When bombing raids in the area did start, the various factories and docks received quite a severe pounding. The local residents, many of whom had moved from the slums of the East End of London some years before the war, also suffered. Not only did they get a large number of the high explosive bombs intended for the factories and docks, but during the Blitz they had to endure the nightly danger of having homes set on fire by a deluge of incendiary bombs. I heard of many housewives, whose husbands were in the forces, who saved their homes from flames several times over all by themselves, as there were more fires than the ARP and fire service could deal with. There was a great deal of unsung and unrecorded heroism during this time when the people united in their battle against a common adversary. Although there was very severe bombing around the docks and East End of London, the people of Dagenham and other industrial suburbs also took a heavy hammering which rarely gets mentioned in the history books.

In my new job I met the public directly and I liked that aspect of the work greatly, but joining the Ministry of Food for a period which extended to more than three years nearly drove me mad. I have always found that the Civil Service and I don't mix very comfortably at all. When I was told that everything had to be completed in triplicate and that I had to ask half a dozen people above me before I made a decision that I could have made when I was ten years of age, I can understand why it costs so much to run. A large proportion of it, even in wartime, was bureaucracy for the sake of bureaucracy.

But I got on with the job; in any case I preferred it to being cooped up below ground, and I met many other people. It was actually a very responsible position. Not only did we have to issue the ration books when the scheme started, but we had to deal with emergency coupons for those who had been bombed out, special coupons for those travelling away and to investigate the authenticity of claims from people who said theirs had been lost or destroyed. Of course, it was essential during war time, but I could never really understand why the post-war government continued with rationing for such a long time when every other European country had dispensed with it so quickly.

To prevent myself from becoming just another Civil Servant blindly dispensing pieces of paper, I continued with outside activities as much as possible. With Claude Dyer and other friends I travelled all over the South East of England and throughout East Anglia giving shows to the troops in the evenings and at weekends.

Before leaving the Civic Centre I also became involved with the Women's Voluntary Service (now the Women's Royal Voluntary Service). The District Organiser for the WVS in Dagenham was a local Councillor, Mrs Lillian Evans. She was a very down-to-earth, hard bitten, practical, sensible woman with a heart of gold. I greatly admired her and could well understand why she supported the Labour Party. Her husband had marched from South Wales to London in the hunger marches of the 1920s, and later on when he died of tuberculosis, Mrs Evans had brought up six young children by herself. She had known what it was to be extremely poor, but forgot her party politics and personal prejudices and was willing to do anything in her power and work with anyone to help win the war.

It was under Mrs Evans' leadership that a voluntary body called the 'Housewives' Service' was set up in the Borough and she asked me to take charge of it. I worked as head of that service right through the war. It was a wonderful idea devised by the WVS to help those areas most likely to be bombed. Unfortunately, this also rarely receives a mention in any of the records of the Second World War. The procedure was to identify those districts which were most likely to suffer from bombing and then in each road, or at regular intervals, to have a house with a spare room which could be devoted and prepared to deal with any casualties that occurred within that section. It was community involvement and community care before those expressions became devalued by self-seeking politicians. But its purpose was clear. The intention was that if anyone was bombed out of their home they had somewhere in the immediate neighbourhood where they could gather. This enabled families to check on who was missing and assisted the authorities in deciding how much temporary accommodation was required for rehousing those who had lost their homes.

It was a splendid idea and was very effective in some districts. However, within Dagenham we found it almost impossible to be able to site a centre in each street where we would have liked. This was in no way due to people not wanting to co-operate, but because of the overcrowding in the district. By this time many of the children had returned from the first bout of evacuation and many of the families were large, whilst most of the houses only possessed two or three bedrooms. In addition to this, some of the tenants had taken in relations who had been bombed out from their homes in Stepney, Poplar and West Ham, where the devastation had been most severe. But set up the service we did, although it was only on a skeleton scale in places, and where it existed it worked and worked well, thanks to the many unsung people who made the sacrifices so essential to the success of any form of voluntary service.

During various odd moments I also managed to find enough time to start the local section of the Women's Junior Air Corps. This led eventually to a number of local girls joining the Royal Air Force on a permanent basis.

The various activities kept me busy and lively, but after more than three years in the Dagenham Food Office I became very weary of the eternal battle of trying to cut through the red tape that had been knotted so tightly by Whitehall. I often had the feeling that my superiors did not wish to take the responsibility of making decisions that required action. If they made a decision it was usually 'No', particularly to any suggestion for improvement, because that answer meant they had to do nothing. Rather than say 'Yes', they would say 'I am in no position to decide, the idea must go to higher authority.' So either way the idea was generally killed and it was in any case pushed off the superior's desk. It was a frustrating life for anyone with any enthusiasm or enterprise and I knew there was a limit to how long I could take it. The great trouble with bureaucracy, the Civil Service, income tax and form filling in general is that it's the small people who suffer. By that I mean those least capable of fighting the bureaucracy are the ones who have to use it the most and are the ones who find themselves filling in the largest number of forms. It is probably in order to confuse these people that most official forms are arranged like a tartan pattern with no two adjacent squares the same size and no square the right size to write anything in with letters larger than a sixteenth of an inch tall. It is the small people who suffer and need the help and support from the rest of us to avoid being squashed by the bureaucrats.

By now, Mrs Evans had become Mayor of the Borough of Dagenham and in addition to her WVS work visited many of the local factories on official business. I had told her that I had reached the stage at which I just had to change my job for my own sanity and I would be applying for a transfer. 1 could not just walk out and take any other job because at that time I could have been directed to work anywhere in the country where I might have been needed.

During one of her visits she met the managing director of a local engineering company that was involved with making armaments as part of the war effort. She told him that she was very concerned that she might lose the organiser of her Housewives' Service, who was so bored and threatening to leave the Food Office. She asked him if it was at all possible for him to find a job for me in his factory because as I was mobile, single and with no ties, I could be moved anywhere away from Dagenham, and she had no wish to lose me from my WVS work. He told her he would be happy to try and find me a job if I would go along to see him. As the company was engaged on very important military production he anticipated no difficulty about arranging the transfer if I was suitable for the job he had in mind.

So a few days later along I went to meet this very helpful managing director. His first words to me were, 'I understand the local WVS don't want you to leave the area.'

'Well, really I don't want to leave the district' I replied, deciding to be as straightforward as possible. 'I've got my own flat here and don't want to lose that, but am completely fed up with my job in the Food Office.' He smiled and said, 'You don't like the Civil Service then?'

'No, I don't' I replied forcefully, forgetting that his company probably had very close ties with sections of the Civil Service through its military contracts.

But my answer did not seem to put him off because he followed it up by asking me what experience I had and what I could do. So I had to admit that the only other work I had done was to run the wholesale department of a very large firm of motor agents and that I had had no formal office training. Finally he said, 'Very well, I'll arrange for you to come and work for me and we'll sort out the matter of the official transfer.'

It wasn't until I left the interview that I realised that he hadn't specified what the job was to be, other than to say that I would be directly responsible to him. Still wondering what I was letting myself in for this time, I gave a month's notice to the Ministry of Food and once the time had elapsed left to join the Sterling Engineering Company, who developed and manufactured the Sterling Machine Gun. I had no idea that this would be the cause of me taking up the welfare work which was to become my major interest and occupation for the remainder of my working life.

As soon as I arrived I was pitchforked into a fund raising campaign called *Salute the Soldier Week.* In many ways this was rather funny, because I had become involved in working for the National Savings movement some time earlier and had been responsible for sending out the letters to companies asking them to assist in this particular scheme. Having joined the engineering company and with no defined duties I was immediately delegated to organise the fund raising activities within the factory. This really was no mean task as the war was very much at its height and the factory was working non-stop to produce parts for bombs and breach blocks for guns twenty-four hours a day, seven days a week. But the fund raising was very successful and my interest in the National Savings movement eventually led to me becoming chief organiser in the Dagenham area until it was disbanded more than thirty years later, when savings stamps were foolishly discontinued.

However, the initial result of my taking part in *Salute the Soldier Week* was that I had the free run of the whole factory and had the opportunity to meet everyone from floor sweepers to directors; something that would normally take a new member of staff several years to achieve, even within a small factory. I also built up an encyclopaedic knowledge of the factory, its layout, its rest areas, its organisation and its work. For the greater part I got on well with all the people with whom I came into contact and quickly gained their confidence. They wanted the fund raising in the factory to be a success and thanks to their generosity we made a very substantial contribution to the war effort.

This success virtually dictated what my role in the factory was going to be for the next twenty-five years.

The managing director heard of the success of the savings week and sent for me to come and see him. I had no idea what he had in mind, but couldn't have been more surprised when he said, 'As you know, we are without a welfare officer. We did have one, but we haven't at present and I consider it essential that we get one. I think you are just the right person to do the job. Will you take it?'

I was completely staggered. I hadn't the remotest idea what it meant or what it involved. I assumed his offer of the job was intended as a compliment but the idea of becoming a welfare officer in a factory was something that had never crossed my mind. It was not a well-known occupation in those days and the title could cover a multitude of things. So I plucked up the courage and asked him what he meant by welfare, and will always remember his words. He said, 'I'll tell you what it means. It means common sense and you've got plenty of it. Now go and get on with it.'

So, once again I was thrown in at the deep end to deal with such problems as working conditions, protective clothing, food, the everyday issuing and laundering of overalls and generally looking after anything that affected the welfare and work of the people in the factory. I found it was really my life's work, it was something I knew immediately when I started that I would always love doing it and never tire of it. I'd rather deal with people than anything in the world. There is something very special at being able to help people in difficulties and there is no such thing as two people alike, they are all different. I do think that workers in the field of welfare do have to have some special ability or personality. At the same time I must emphasise that welfare, and particularly industrial welfare, is a job enough in itself. It should not be mixed or confused with personnel management. I found my own feet in the work very quickly and soon felt that I was doing a useful job of work, although the problems I had to sort out were frequently unpleasant, sometimes horrifying and occasionally amusing.

I soon found that the secret of the good relationship which a welfare officer has to attain with the people in the factory is to remember that you are the liaison between the management and the employee. Whilst you are there to give the maximum assistance to the person who has asked for your help or guidance, you have at the same time a major loyalty to the company employing you. As a welfare officer it is your job to lighten the mental load of the worried worker to enable him or her to do a job for which the management are paying. I think people often fail to appreciate that if a personal, mental or financial problem can be cleared up for an employee, they are able to give better attention to their work and are less likely to make mistakes or turn out poor quality workmanship. Also, a person who is worried and not concentrating on his or her work is much more likely to make a slip that could cause an accident leading to someone being injured or even killed. So that, indirectly, the welfare officer may not only assist in maintaining production but also in reducing the accident figures.

I frequently found in the early days that the machine operators in the factory did not have sufficient confidence in me as their 'new welfare officer' to actually approach me about their problems. I would get to learn of a particular problem as a result of the foreman who would take me on one side and tell me he was worried about a particular woman whose work was not up to her normal standard and was turning out so much rubbish that she was costing the firm money.

In these cases I would have a chat with the woman and often found that she was worked up over what to most people would be quite a trivial matter. It would have arisen from her receiving a letter from the local authority, or one of the ministries or from her child's school, which she didn't understand. And, rather than try to deal with it she would put it in the traditional East End filing cabinet: behind the clock. I often thought that the selling of clocks in Dagenham must have been a very profitable business because everything: bills, football pool coupons, provident cheques, rent books and letters, all seemed to finish up on the mantelpiece filed behind the clock. Once filed they were rarely looked at except when the clock was wound up. It was a marvellous filing cabinet, but the offending missive did not, like the time, vanish never to return. The inevitable would happen and in a few weeks would come a reminder or a final demand or even a summons. It was at this stage that I would find myself involved because of the deterioration in the quality of that person's work at the factory. All too often it was something that could have been sorted out in a tenth of the time if I had known earlier.

What I did find out very early on – doing as I had been instructed and using my common sense – was that under no circumstances should I point out to the person how stupid they had been. It was clear that any form of recrimination or criticism would make them close up like a clam. Then they would go and tell their friends how unhelpful I had been. Diplomacy was essential at all times, so I would tell them how to fill in the form, where to take it, the best way to apologise to the bureaucrat for taking so long in dealing with it, and generally clearing the air. If it was a particularly difficult problem I would deal with the whole thing myself, and usually found that the officials were rarely prepared to try and intimidate me in the way they often did with the general public.

In all this time I had no formal training in welfare work, I learnt it by hard experience. I greatly regret not having done some academic work to back up my firsthand experience, but do not believe that an academic training is in any way the be-all-and-end-all for something as complicated as human relations. People who train for welfare work these days seem to have courses which are heavily weighted in the wrong direction. Instead of being three-quarters theory and one-quarter practical it should be one-quarter theory and three-quarters practical.

All too often, with all this theory on human psychology and personal relationships the newly qualified welfare officer tends to forget that instead of trying to be a tame psychoanalyst the real job is to help. In many ways the first basis of success as a welfare officer is to be reliable. If you promise someone you will help and you fail to carry out that promise just once they will feel that they are unable to trust you and will never come to you for help again. They will say, 'She doesn't understand or want to help, it's no good asking her', and will probably turn to someone else less able to assist them properly. As a welfare officer you are their safety net, their shoulder to cry on, their father (or mother) confessor and the repository of their secrets. At no time can you afford to break their confidence.

The most unpleasant side of my work was when a death or bad injury occurred and I had the job of notifying the next of kin. The reaction to the news was always totally unpredictable. It was often the small, frail people that seemed to stand up to the bad news best of all. Almost as if they were no stranger to bad news and accepted it as part of life. At other times the most solid, hard person would crumple up in front of you when told someone in the family had been hurt. It was a difficult task to carry out in a considerate and understanding manner, but one in which I had had firsthand experience and still carried the mental scars from the loss of my father in the *Titanic* disaster.

The first time I encountered death in the factory and had the dreadful task of passing on the news was only a short time after I started the job. I went into work fairly early in the morning whenever possible so that people did not have to wait to lunchtime before they were able to see me if they needed help. On this particular day I had no sooner got through the gates than someone rushed up to me and told me that a fairly elderly man, who was well liked in the factory, had suffered a seizure while putting on his working overalls immediately before coming into the factory. Although the ambulance had arrived very quickly he had died on his way to hospital before his family had been informed.

Now the responsibility became mine. I had the job of notifying the widow and of clearing up as far as possible the paperwork concerned with the death of an employee. This included everything involving his pension rights, social security payments and the myriad of small details that arise as soon as anyone dies. Not the least of these was to ensure that his family would not be left for weeks without any income.

In this instance it all turned out to be more difficult than anyone had expected. The wife actually took the news of the death reasonably well, but it very quickly created a great deal of unhappiness for her which could only be partially sorted out. The problems arose because they had not been legally married. The poor woman was not English and they had gone through what she had thought was a correct form of marriage but was actually totally invalid. The complications and ramifications that caused seemed endless because she couldn't apply for probate or letters of administration and had no real right to make the necessary funeral arrangements. Most of the immediate problems were eventually sorted out, but the poor woman was so upset at finding her marriage void, and she was so lonely, that she committed suicide about a year later. That was one of the most unhappy things I ever had to deal with.

In that last case the death of the man had actually taken place just outside the factory, but when a death occurs within a place of work the Coroner's Officer has to be called to the scene of death before the body can be moved. This is probably in case there is any blame to be apportioned to the company, as would be the case in a death arising from an industrial accident.

A situation like this occurred the second time I had a death on my hands, when one of our workers collapsed and died on a Friday afternoon. Unfortunately it took a long time to get anyone from the Coroner's office and the nurse and I were left in the factory for hours after everyone had gone home. It was the middle of a bitterly cold winter and we became almost as stiff and as cold as the body we were guarding before we were able to transfer the responsibility to the appropriate authorities.

Fortunately there was often a more humorous side that came out even when tragedy was on the doorstep, and frequently it was the children that helped to put my feet back on the ground.

I had one instance when I was told that one of our workers had had to go home because his wife had been whisked off to hospital. I went round to the house to see if I could help and was able to find a neighbour to come in to keep an eye on the young children during the afternoon. However, she could not stay very late as she had her own family to attend to later on. So I arranged to come back when the older children were due home from school and to get their tea for them and prepare the youngest for bed while the husband was at the hospital.

Food was of prime importance to this group of youngsters and it was not until after tea that the youngest boy, a little devil of less than five years old, said 'Can you tell me where my Mummy is?'

I don't believe in being unnecessarily evasive with children and answered, 'Your Mummy has gone to the doctor because she isn't very well, but she will soon be better and come home to look after you.'

That seemed to satisfy all of them and a short time after the youngest one asked if he could have a bath. That in itself should have made me suspicious that there was something being cooked up as little boys don't usually ask to be cleaned up so readily. But, not knowing what I was letting myself in for I agreed and went upstairs to run the bath. The small lad soon followed and quickly undressed and hopped into the water. No sooner had he done so than some form of telepathy was transmitted downstairs. I heard a scurrying in the kitchen and then up the stairs, three at a time, bounded their enormous dog. As I stood open mouthed it ran straight past me and without stopping leapt straight into the bath with the young boy.

The child had obviously been longing to have the dog in the bath for ages and he had taken his one chance with both hands. I didn't have the heart, or courage, to try and take the dog out, but I don't think either of them finished up any cleaner as most of the water went on the floor. The children obviously kept the episode to themselves because their father never made any comment to me about the dog in the bath. But in future cases like that I tried to make sure that I was told clearly what children had in mind before I agreed to what, on the surface, seemed harmless.

Most people are very grateful when you do anything to help them, and generally I find that the smaller the problem you have assisted in sorting out the greater the gratitude and the warmer the thanks you receive for it. Because of this, the rare case of ingratitude tends to hurt rather more deeply than one really expects.

I had a rare example of this with one particular man whom I had helped tremendously, not only in the factory but also outside normal office hours, during a period when he had suffered severe personal difficulties. I thought I had become very close to that man and his family and was quite amazed when he came into my office in a blazing temper complaining about the increased cost of a cup of tea in the firm. There had been every justification for the increase and even at the higher price our canteen prices were lower than in most other local factories.

I spent a great deal of time pointing out to him the various costs that were incurred in making and serving the tea and thought I had convinced him that he was being unfair with his criticism of the company and that there really was no case for me to take up with the management. He went away apparently placated by what I had said. But later that day I was told there was a noisy disturbance in one of the machine shops – there I found the man holding forth to his colleagues, telling them what a bad welfare officer I was and not to come to me with any problems. I thought that would be the end of it and things would return to normal once the men went back to their machines. But the next day I found this selfsame man had decided he was going to get value for money and was expecting the tea girl to fill up a brand new pint mug for the price of a cup of tea.

It was the type of situation all welfare officers dislike. If you do nothing you are considered weak, and if you fail to keep a sense of proportion you can precipitate industrial action that could cost the price of millions of cups of tea.

It was not easy to reason with the man. 'You know perfectly well that isn't a cup of tea, it's a pint mug' I said firmly, knowing that all the workers were looking and wondering how I was going to handle this situation. 'If you want a pint of tea you may have it, I don't mind in the slightest.' Looks of surprise went round, surely the welfare officer wasn't climbing down so easily.

'But if you do, you will pay for a pint of tea' I continued, 'I see no reason at all why you should expect to get a pint of tea for the price of a cup of tea. I don't think that's right or fair to the others, so have what you like in the future, but you will pay for it.' With that I walked away well knowing that his fellow workers would not let him have extra tea at their expense.

It was the first instance of how ungrateful people can be and the depth of his ingratitude appalled me. I had always remembered how grateful the *Titanic* survivors had been to anyone for even the smallest kindness that they met after the tragedy that I had not at that stage prepared myself for that man's reaction. But over the years I became inured to it and a little less sensitive. Despite his reaction, I knew that most of what I did was greatly appreciated by the employees and management alike and I enjoyed every minute of my work. I enjoyed it to the extent that even when I later became a magistrate I made sure that I was still available to the workers every day. And on the days when I was due at court I would make a point of being at the factory especially early that day to ensure that any problems were dealt with before I left for court.

Having changed my job twice in my early working years I then stayed with this particular engineering company for twenty-five years and saw the change-over from military production in wartime, through the difficulties of the late 1940s to the early 1950s back to normal engineering and the development of the problems created by increased automation. These were all difficulties which the company managed to weather with no major industrial disturbances. I like to think that my welfare work contributed to the long-term harmony that prevailed within that factory.

Now that my singing days are long over I look back to those years with many pleasant memories because of the wide variety of experiences and opportunities they covered.

There is, of course, a great deal of difference between singing to a Sunday audience on the *Titanic* and singing choral works and operatic arias in large auditoria. In all instances, however, it is of considerable importance to be able to project your voice well in order that the person at the back can hear just as well as the person at the front. I am horrified at the way in which so many modem singers clasp a microphone as near to their mouths as possible in order to be heard. This suggests to me that most of them have never had a singing lesson in their lives and do not understand how to get the best from their voices. Even now when I am speaking to large audiences I decline to use a microphone. Many are the chairmen I have disconcerted who have spent ages playing with plugs, switches and wires only to be told that I can speak better without a microphone than they can with one.

I was fortunate enough to have an excellent singing teacher who taught me all she knew about voice projection, pitch and elocution. As a result I could undertake a wide range of singing engagements. On many of these I accompanied Claude Dyer, who had acquired a national reputation for his own singing of oratorios including 'Elijah' and 'Messiah'.

The engagements we accepted were varied and we were as likely to find ourselves on a town hall stage as in the ballroom of a major hotel or a small local theatre. But it was great fun and I always enjoyed it wherever the concert was held. One of the interesting features about that type of semi-professional work was the way in which I kept meeting a number of other artists fairly regularly at different places.

I frequently found myself at the same venue as Jack Warner. That was long before he took the part of PC George Dixon in the film *The Blue Lamp* and became identified as the policeman from the Dock Green Police Station. That film was itself a landmark in the making of popular police films and stories in Great Britain which expanded into the many lucrative police series on television. But few people remember Jack Warner as the versatile entertainer he was before he made his career in the role that did so much over many years to improve relations between the public and the police. Jack's success in *Dixon of Dock Green* only came many years after he had already established himself as a performer nationally known for his songs and character acting. I find that people under the age of forty tend to remember Jack for his 'Dixon' role and know nothing about the route he took up the entertainment ladder, or of the many years he worked before anything like success really came. But he was well known by the troops in the Second World War for his comedy sketches and wartime film parts.

Over the years I remained a close friend of Jack and his wife, Molly, and often stayed with them in their house near the sea in Kent. My visits were made even more enjoyable if we persuaded Jack to tell us about *The Bunger Upper Of Rat Holes,* or got him to perform some other of his earlier cabaret and radio material. He was a very versatile entertainer and for over forty years was continually successful on stage, screen, radio and television. I shall never forget that at the funeral, after he died, the centrepiece was a beautiful, large flower arrangement made to look like the traditional blue lamp which can still be seen outside some of the older Police Stations. It was a fitting farewell to a much loved person.

Jack's two sisters, Elsie and Doris Waters, were also great fun to work with and their character presentation of *Gert and Daisy* gave pleasure to millions for many years, especially during and immediately after the Second World War. When my voice was probably at its best I was fortunate enough to be invited to be a guest in one of their *Working Parties* broadcast during wartime.

One of the outstanding characteristics of all three of the Waters family was their humility. They never sought to deny or cover up

their origins in the East End of London. I well remember on one
occasion when Elsie and Doris were doing a show from a theatre in
that part of London one of the BBC staff was being highly critical
about the intelligence of the people making up the audience. The
two sisters rounded on him, saying, 'We come from this area and
we know these people. They are the salt of the earth, and don't you
forget it!' To them the important thing was that they were back
home and performing for a grateful public – what more could any
artiste want?

Another entertainer of enormous character was Arthur Askey.
He was always one of my favourite comedians ever since I first
met him in the early 1930s. It was an evening when we were both
due to perform in cabaret at a Masonic ladies' night in central
London. Arthur was always a perfect gentleman and did not resort
to crudity or unpleasantness to achieve his humour. He was a
natural comic and the jokes and laughs bubbled out of him in a
continuous stream.

On this evening I was due to sing some of my ballads and he
was to entertain with a number of his ditties. We were both due to
follow a man who was at that time a leading comic. Shortly after
the man had started his act, which we could hear from the artists'
dressing room, Arthur got up from his seat, walked across to the
open door and immediately shut it. It was awfully hot in the room
and I asked him why he had closed the door.

> I feel that a young lady like you would not want to hear the
> type of humour that comedian is putting over, that's why I
> closed the door.

He said in reply to my question.

In these modern progressive days that probably sounds a little
prudish, but to me it was an indication of the consideration that
was always shown by 'Big Hearted' Arthur Askey.

It was many years before I saw Arthur again, and by that time I
think he had forgotten the young singer he had saved from a few
blushes. But one weekend in 1973 when I was staying with Jack
and Molly Warner they said, 'Eva, we have a surprise for you. We
are taking you out this evening to somewhere special.'

Needless to say that whetted my appetite and tried all that
Saturday to find out where we were going, without success. Then
at 7 p.m. we all piled into Jack's car and off we went, with me still
wondering what it was after all these years that Jack and Molly

could produce that would be a surprise. But a surprise it was. We went to a theatre in Margate to see ... Arthur Askey. Jack said, 'You have been raving about Arthur all these years so I thought we would take this opportunity of his visit to this area for you to see him in a live performance.'

That was a marvellous evening. Arthur's performance was superb. He went through many of the outstanding items in his repertoire including his famous *Bee Song.* At that time he was into his seventies but remained active and nimble and could hold an audience without the support of backing groups, amplifiers or other artists. A genuine entertainer in the best sense.

We all went to see him backstage at the end of the performance and Jack, who knew him well, introduced me to him once again. He was quite surprised that I should have remembered our first meeting as a result of what was, to him, such a minor action. Following that second meeting I later received an autographed copy of Arthur Askey's own story of his battle to the top of what is a very difficult and demanding profession.

The coming of the Second World War in 1939 had meant that my own singing became rather fragmented and my engagements took a different form. On two occasions, the engineering factory where I was the welfare officer, was selected as the venue for the BBC radio lunch-time programme *Works Wonders,* in which the performers were drawn from the factory employees. Ours was quite a small company and most people knew about my spare time singing. As a result, I was asked to sing on the programme while it was broadcast from the factory canteen. The fact that I was asked to sing in a second show after the war I felt was a great compliment and showed that despite the difficult acoustics I must have performed reasonably well the first time. Certainly the compere of that show, Brian Johnston, made us all feel very much at ease and it was no surprise to me that he went on to become such a success with his relaxed style as both a commentator and an author. I came to know Brian as a personal friend and on a couple of occasions after the War persuaded him to come to functions in Chadwell Heath. I was very upset by his death early in 1994.

One advantage of taking part in *Works Wonders* was that I was able to obtain a gramophone record of the radio broadcast. It was one of the few opportunities I had to listen to my own singing when it was at its best. After the war ended in 1945 *Works Wonders* was replaced by *Workers' Playtime* and the first programme came from the Sterling Engineering Factory. I was able to obtain the autographs of all the stars including Avril Angers and the Western Brothers, Kenneth and George.

During the Second World War the government made every effort to provide adequate entertainment for the troops both overseas and at home. To assist in this work a group of semi-professionals, including me, formed a Concert Party to travel around East Anglia and the Home Counties to the various camps and defence posts. The booking and travelling arrangements were all made by the War Office, and we were delighted to find that we were entitled to a special allocation of clothing coupons to help provide our costumes. Such coupons were like gold dust and had to be guarded with our lives as well as being fully accounted for because the black market value was substantial.

In many instances when we went on our trips to gun sites we had no idea of the location as this was usually kept a secret. All signposts on the roads had been removed in order to confuse any invaders or German spies – with the result that the home population was even more confused, as they rarely carried maps. To avoid getting lost it was always necessary for us to meet an escort at a prearranged point, who would then lead us to our final destination. We would often travel for hours with shielded headlamps, along unlit roads behind the faint glimmer of a motorcycle rear lamp into remote country areas. Most of the routes would be through narrow country lanes and dark woods, sometimes finishing up at an airfield or at a fortification on the coast, but it was nearly always at a very isolated spot. Despite the strain of the journey our concerts were always well received and we felt we really helped to relieve the gloom a little during those depressing years.

Needless to say, our trips to the wilds of England were not without incident!

Our very first show as the Concert Party was at a troop camp at Lippetts Hill, in the heart of Epping Forest. The stage had been hastily improvised from a number of planks supported on beer crates. There were no curtains, but somehow they had procured a lovely full-sized grand piano for us. Our accompanist sat down to strike some chords to get things started. He put his feet on the pedals – which promptly fell to pieces. Then as we trooped in together for our opening chorus the stage collapsed underneath us. The soldiers roared with laughter, no doubt thinking it was all part of the act. We finally came through our initiation by dispensing with the stage and using the piano without the benefit of the pedals.

Pianos frequently created problems for us as we were entirely dependent upon what was provided. Sometimes there was no piano, often the one provided was out of tune, and sometimes the keys would stick so that a series of important notes would get missed out. On one classic occasion our pianist, with his monocle jammed in his eye, was trying out some bars before a show and I called across to him, 'Robbie, what's the piano like?'

'I think I can say its parents were never married', came the quick reply, accompanied by a discordant sample from the hammers.

Dressing rooms had to be taken as they were found – and some were so dreadful they would have been better permanently lost.

One of our venues was a gun-site near to Waltham Abbey. But when we arrived we discovered it had been hit by a bomb and our accommodation had been destroyed. However, the show had to go on and we were offered a small hut as an alternative dressing room. That seemed perfectly all right until we found that we had been preceded by the delivery of the camp's meat ration. We shared our dressing room with undressed carcasses of beef dripping blood around us. It was nearly enough to turn us all into vegetarians overnight.

Facilities were often crude, to say the least. Sometimes there were no proper dressing rooms and we would have to change behind curtains at the side of the stage only a whisper's distance from the seats in the front row. On one occasion we found there was no exit from the 'dressing room' except on to the stage. So once the performance was under way we were trapped until the end of the show. The only provision for our physical needs during this time was a large galvanised bucket, and what none of us realised until half-way through the evening was that every time we used the bucket the continuous metallic tinkle rang clearly through the curtain to a highly amused audience. To accompany the 'music' and to cover its sound, one of our company sang *What Are the Wild Waves Saying?* As far as we were concerned, they were saying far too much!

If we were likely to be away for more than one evening, the War Office would arrange overnight accommodation for us. Sometimes we would carry out a weekend tour, leaving for a show on Friday evening and not getting home until late Sunday night. As our party was anything from eight to a dozen people, such trips normally meant long journeys in a huge, uncomfortable van provided by the War Office.

Late one Friday night we arrived at our weekend accommodation on the Essex coast to be greeted somewhat dourly by the proprietress. We had thought we were going to be lucky that night as 'the powers that be' had booked us into a guest-house right on the sea front. Although it was in a military closed area it was permitted to remain open because the NAAFI had taken the ground floor and official guests, such as ourselves, were regularly booked in for short visits.

However, the landlady of the establishment did not appear to appreciate our late arrival. Our party, which numbered ten on this occasion, included two married couples, two girls who were prepared to share a room, and four of us requiring single rooms. We were taken upstairs and led to our accommodation – five double bedrooms. The protests were short and sharp. 'We booked three double and four single rooms, not these.' we all said at once.

'Ten people means five rooms to me. I don't care who sleeps with who, and I'm sure none of you do! I know your sort, all you actors sleep with each other!' she said in a tone of voice that implied we were not the first entertainers to visit her august establishment.

It took quite a time to persuade her that we meant what we said and really did not wish to share each other's beds. Finally, she said we could damned well sleep where we liked if we made up our own beds. So at 1.30 a.m. we were roaming around the guest house opening bedroom doors – finding some already occupied – and pulling blankets, sheets and pillowcases out of cupboards to make up the additional beds, all the time being carefully watched by the aggressive woman who obviously thought we were going to steal all her best linen. Eventually we got to bed in the early hours of Saturday morning.

We did two shows on the Saturday and the Sunday, returning to our 'hotel' each night hoping that no one else had usurped our rooms having been assured that guests could sleep where they liked and with whom!

At least, during that particular weekend we had been reasonably fed, but that was not always the case. On one trip to Cranleigh in Surrey, almost everything possible went wrong. To begin with the War Office had been unable to provide any transport and Claude Dyer had borrowed a huge limousine with pale grey upholstery in order to get us to our destination. As a result, the journey was rather more comfortable than usual. But as most of us had not eaten since early in the day, we were starving and exhausted by the end of the evening performance, fully expecting the normal hospitalities to be extended to us. We were amazed to find that nobody had thought about providing us with any form of a meal after the show.

We piled into our beautiful car as quickly as possible and Claude drove off immediately, only to stop at the first fish and chip shop he could find. On the way home we revelled in the pleasure of eating fried fish and chips straight from the paper; never has the British national dish tasted so nice. We gorged ourselves full, getting grease all over ourselves as well as over the seats of the car. It was marvellous – and the car was filled with the smell which clung fast to the grey upholstery. Claude had a difficult job explaining the odour which remained when he returned it next day as it was due to be used immediately for a wedding. I often wonder if some poor bride finished up with her wedding gown smelling of our fish and chips!

Our concert party broke up at the end of the war, but a smaller group of us formed a vocal quartet to give recitals around London and South East England. This was very similar to what I had been doing before the war and we had many invitations to sing. Amongst the places we visited was the chapel at Wormwood Scrubs Prison. While I was singing there I little dreamt that years later I would be attending in an official capacity on the Board of Visitors.

My singing career came to an end when I was fifty-seven and lost my singing voice. Over a short period of time I found I was becoming very tired, and for some reason my voice didn't flow in the way it used to. In fact, for the first time in my life it became hard work to sing and eventually I felt I had to turn down engagements. After a careful medical examination it was diagnosed that I had myxoedema – which in its worst forms not only causes tiredness but also leads to nails breaking, hair falling out and a puffy complexion. It meant that my thyroid gland was giving up working and the only treatment was a regular dose of tablets containing thyroxin. Fortunately, it had been diagnosed early enough to save my speaking voice, but my singing days were over.

It is difficult to explain how great a loss this was to me. Singing had given me enormous pleasure as well as the opportunity to travel widely and to meet many other artists and entertainers, and now that part of my life was over. I consoled myself with the thought that I could still play my piano and derive pleasure from hearing other people sing. I was very pleased to find that my speaking voice was still strong enough to enable me to give talks about my career as a welfare officer and about the *Titanic* disaster, which by this time seemed to be increasing in public interest. As a result, my speaking engagements increased and helped to fill the great gap in my life caused by a small gland that would not function properly.

9

IT'S A HARD BENCH

The bus I was on crawled along from Chadwell Heath to Seven Kings and I was horrified to see that the conductor had unclipped his ticket machine and put it into his little brown box. I knew from bitter experience that meant the bus was going to stop halfway to change crews – with a further inevitable delay. So I asked him what time we were likely to get to Stratford. When he said he was going off-duty and the bus would have to slow down because it was running early I became very agitated, knowing that I was already late.

Being an understanding and kindly person he came across and said, 'Why are you getting in such a "two and eight" love?'

I explained that I was in a state because I was due at Stratford Court and was terrified of being late. He gave me a most superior look and said somewhat loftily, 'Stratford Court? You don't want to worry about them old buggers – keep 'em waiting!'

With that type of advice I didn't have the nerve to tell him that I was the newest of the 'old buggers' on the local bench and had been told that I should arrive early on my first day in order to be able to see around the courts before proceedings started for the day.

That all took place in 1956 and to this day I do not know who recommended that I should be considered to become a Justice of the Peace. When I was appointed to the bench the procedure was far different from what it is now. For instance, it is not uncommon to see items in the local newspapers informing the readers that a particular county wishes to increase the number of magistrates and asking people who wish to be considered to apply. This method of involving the public directly arose partly because a number of 'progressive' and 'enlightened' people complained that the existing JPs were not representative of the community structure. If this were ever to be the case it would mean that we would have to include a representative number of burglars, rapists and arsonists, as well as a representative number of illiterates and people who do not speak English. For this reason alone JPs are not and cannot be representative of a cross-section of the populace. They do need to be of above average intelligence, with an above average dedication to their duty and a desire to administer justice without fear or favour. Being working class, middle class or anything else has nothing whatsoever to do with the responsibilities of the post.

When I was considered for the bench it was not possible for you to put yourself forward in any way and had you tried to do so that would have been a sure guarantee that you would not become a JP. For me it all started with a letter I received one day in the autumn of 1955 which just asked me if I would like to be considered for appointment as one of Her Majesty's Justices of the Peace. I couldn't believe that anyone could seriously think about me taking on such a job when I had never been inside a police court in my life.

I thought about the matter for a little time, considering carefully how much time it would require and how I would be able to carry on the full-time welfare work at the engineering company. I still couldn't believe that such an honour could come my way. But I decided that it was the type of work I would enjoy doing and I felt that my welfare work had by now given me a very good insight into human nature. So, still with some apprehension in my mind, I replied saying I would be prepared to serve.

The anticlimax was horrible. I didn't hear anything further for months, and the original letter had said that if I mentioned the matter to anyone or talked about it in any way I would hear no more. So I was totally unable to unburden myself to anyone and went around with the secret bursting inside me for week after week.

It was not until one snowy day in the New Year that I had a second letter informing me that my application was being considered and asking me to meet with one of the Deputy Lieutenants of the County of Essex to discuss the work and responsibilities of a magistrate. When the day came I found I was one of three aspirants being considered. It was not really an interview, more a polite form of grilling to find out my attitude to life, what my general views on society were and how I felt people developed and reacted to circumstances. During all this I was trying to act as naturally as possible, but it was very difficult not to think to myself that I had sometimes said the wrong thing. At the end of it all the Deputy Lieutenant said, 'Miss Hart, I imagine you realise that I have been assessing you and taking great note of all your remarks. I cannot tell you at this stage whether or not you will be appointed a JP, but you will hear from us in due course in any case.'

So once again I had to keep my secret bottled up for weeks on end. And right through February, March and April I waited anxiously, searching my mail each day for that special envelope that never seemed to arrive. Then, just when I had given up hope, the letter came saying I had been approved and was to be sworn in at the Shire Hall in Chelmsford on 30 May 1956. That was one of the greatest days of my life. I took the very solemn oath to serve my Queen and Country as a Justice of the Peace without fear or favour and to administer justice. Yes, I was proud to become the possessor of those two letters JP, and very, very conscious of the great responsibility that goes with them.

The bench to which I was appointed at Stratford was one of the largest in Great Britain, being the Becontree Petty Sessional Division covering Leyton, Leytonstone, Walthamstow, Woodford, Wanstead, Ilford, Barking and Dagenham. It was so large that within a short time of my appointment we were provided with another court house at Barking. I am sure that was not just to accommodate me.

My time was shared equally between the old and the new court. The normal rota required attendance for one morning each week, but it was quite normal for that morning to extend into the afternoon. As I became more experienced I also became involved with the various subcommittees associated with the bench, and over the years sat on the licensing bench, the betting and gaming bench and the probation aftercare committee. Eventually, I was appointed by the Quarter Sessions (now the Crown Court) to represent my bench at the prisons. So that during almost twenty years as a magistrate I had firsthand experience at nearly all the possible areas of work.

In the early days I had a great deal to learn and for a long time always had to sit with more experienced magistrates in order to benefit from their knowledge. I had not fully realised until I was appointed a JP that there are two types of magistrate. I had become what the press refer to as a lay magistrate, i.e., a magistrate from among the general public with no proper legal training and serving in an unpaid capacity. The other type of magistrate is the stipendiary magistrate who is legally trained, usually a solicitor, and is paid a stipend in his capacity as a Justice. The stipendiary magistrates play a major role in the administration of justice in the country and are of enormous help in assisting the lay magistrates to understand the responsibilities and duties of the work.

Life in the magistrates' court was very varied and we had to deal with all sorts of cases, including legal separations, burglary, motoring offences, non-payment of television licences and shoplifting. One of the responsibilities that arrives in the lap of the new magistrate, almost unnoticed, is the position of chief form signer. I have witnessed forms for ration books, bank signatures, election expense accounts, wills and the never ending passport forms. During the many years after joining the bench I think I must have witnessed at least one form for every member of the population of Dagenham. I have been amazed by the number of people I was supposed to have known (according to what they claimed) for at least three years when they suddenly wanted a passport urgently. I have always wondered if any check is ever made on the authenticity or reliability of people who have witnessed the passport forms for impersonators and illegal immigrants. Yet I have never heard of anyone being charged for providing false evidence of identity! As a magistrate, I was often asked to sign search warrants for the police. This frequently occurred at night-time as I happen to live near a police station. I never felt that this invasion upon the liberty and privacy of the individual should be taken lightly and always tried to ensure that the police had just cause to search the suspected premises. Whilst I did not get housemaid's knee in my work, I did get writer's cramp just signing my name; fortunately, it is short (and sweet)!

The magistrates' courts also deal with the legal side of educational matters as well as crime by young children. That was, however, one part of the work I did not have the opportunity to work in. It is not normally possible to be appointed to the juvenile bench unless you have been sworn in as a JP before your fiftieth birthday, and I was just over the age when appointed. It was something I always regretted, as it left a gap in my practical experience.

An increasing amount of the court's time is taken up by the ever mounting tide of crime committed by teenagers and the sixteen to eighteen age group plays a major part in this. I always found this section of the community particularly interesting to work with and tried to establish what had turned them into petty criminals. In cases involving young people, particularly first offenders, the magistrates are not just concerned with convicting and punishing but often go to great lengths in order to establish the original cause of the downhill drift. Such things as home circumstances, which may include loss of one or both parents, a poor family background or continual moving from one location to another, all had to be taken into consideration. All of these can and do contribute in turning someone to a life of crime, although other factors also have to be counted. In many instances it is possible to reverse this slide by remedial action and guidance at an early stage.

Despite thinking and studying very hard on the problem, I must admit that after having spent twenty years on the bench I still do not understand what makes a vandal. Vandalism is something I just cannot comprehend, and I have encountered some appalling cases in which sports pavilions have been wrecked, schools burnt down and furniture reduced to firewood. I have no doubt at all that the psychiatrists can find all manner of excuses to justify this type of behaviour. Periodically in court we had psychiatric reports on vandals and for the greater part they consisted of a lot of pseudo-scientific claptrap based upon the need of the vandal to express his pent-up feelings because his father had told him off or hit him the day before. To my mind that does not justify the little thug wrecking something that belongs to other members of the community.

The incredible thing is that as a magistrate I found it was almost impossible to obtain a sensible or logical answer from the vandals. Frequently, I asked them, 'Why did you damage this property? Do you know to whom it belongs?'

'No.'

'Then why did you smash all the new windows?'

'Dunnow, I jus' wanned to – for kicks!'

And that is as far as it was possible to get. Even the probation officers, who are experts in establishing the causes of irrational behaviour, told me that they could rarely find out anything that could be called a true justification (if there is any justification at all) for the vandalism. No doubt the origins lie very deep and can be a mixture of boredom, lack of parental guidance, inferiority complex and lack of satisfaction in studies or work. But as a magistrate with a lifetime of dealing with people of all ages I have usually managed to find the answer to most things, but not to vandalism.

The other crime which I found increased dramatically during my time on the bench was that of shoplifting. The advent and expansion of self-service supermarkets has done a great deal to encourage and assist the shoplifter; not that that justifies the crime. The difficulty from the magistrate's point of view is always to differentiate between the professional shoplifter and the person who has picked something up and walked out with it on the spur of the moment. They are two entirely different types of people and over the years I learnt to recognise the true professional who earns his, or her, living at stealing. The courts do try to be lenient and to show tolerance and understanding to the first time shoplifter and to the old-age pensioner trying to get a tin of salmon. But it is now common for the chain store managers to prosecute all shoplifters as a deterrent to other people.

The cases brought against the habitual and professional shoplifters are well justified. These people are very clever and frequently get away with their crimes for a long time before being apprehended. Their display of indignation, shock and bravado in court is usually up to the level of Sir John Gielgud as a performance. Their horror when they eventually receive a prison sentence rather than another fine, because of the record of stealing they have built up, is amazing.

When I sat in judgement on major shoplifting cases I pointed out to the convicted people that they were taking something that belonged to someone else and they were as bad as burglars and housebreakers. They usually became very self-righteous and indignant at this, and one woman actually said to me, 'I haven't committed a crime. The shop will get its money back from insurance, why should they worry if I take something I want without paying for it?'

These people live in a world of their own and have minds which move along a totally twisted and illogical pathway. Just as the vandal fails to appreciate that the property he destroys has to be paid for by the rates and taxes taken from his own salary or that of his parents, so the shoplifter fails to accept that the cost of articles stolen means that the other prices in shops must be higher to compensate for that loss, or the money is recovered by charging higher insurance premiums. In practice, the rest of society has to pay more for its goods and services as a direct result of the actions of the vandal and the shoplifter. Those people who believe that the courts should take a tolerant view of such antisocial behaviour are themselves condoning the action and encouraging the imposition of an ever-increasing burden on the shoulders of the majority of honest and decent people. The vandals and shoplifters are as much parasites on the nation as are the big-time crooks and thieves.

Being a magistrate does not just involve turning up at court one morning or afternoon a week, dashing through a lot of cases, doling out fines and sentences, rubbing your hands with glee at sending down another twenty crooks and basking in all the glory. That is not what being a JP is about.

In the first instance, no decision or sentence should be given lightly or in a hurry, and those people who so frequently criticise the courts for taking their time would be the first to complain if anything involving them was rushed through to their detriment. This is not so say that there is no room for improvement in court procedure; but the essential thing is that people should not be convicted and given police records without due process and great care. It is equally as bad to release a criminal to society when he is guilty as it is to convict an innocent person who should have been found not guilty. So the magistrate must ensure that adequate time is given for the presentation of both sides of the case and if there is any doubt about the ability of the magistrates' court to apply a heavy enough sentence, then the case must be referred to a higher court at which stiffer penalties can be applied for the crime.

The people who appear before the courts are of all types. We had the arrogant people who had been caught out after not paying their television licences for ten years and who then tried to persuade the court that their set was not working at the time. We had the neighbours who were unable to live peacefully next door to each other and had to be bound over to keep the peace. Then there were the motorists who were unable to go out in their cars without tanking themselves up with four or five pints of beer during the journey. Fortunately, the breath test has gone a long way to simplifying most proceedings concerned with drinking and driving. Now all the court has to do is to assure itself that the correct procedure was followed in administering the test at the roadside and in the taking of the blood and urine sample at the police station. If that has all been done satisfactorily then drivers over the 80mg of alcohol per 100ml of blood limit (in Great Britain) are automatically convicted and the sentence, of loss of licence and a fine, imposed. There is now, of course, a close relationship between the laws on drinking and driving in the western world, although higher levels of 100 and 150mg still operate in some other countries.

Some of the people who appeared in front of me in court tried to tell me that they drove better after a few drinks, that they were less hesitant and had not been involved in an accident for years. But the hard fact of the matter is that the chance of being involved in an accident, or finishing up in court and losing your driving licence, increases with increased blood alcohol levels right from the start. If it was only the drivers and their personal property that were put at risk by this irresponsible behaviour then society would not need to be concerned. After all, there is no law against trying to commit suicide. It is, however, the fact that the drinking driver is putting other people, often their family, and other property at risk that necessitates the law and the courts taking action to discourage the drinking driver in an effort to reduce the high level of carnage still occurring on the roads.

There is one group of people who appear in court for whom I always felt particularly sorry. These were the inadequate people who are unable to stand up to the complexities of modem life. They often turned out to be ex-servicemen and women who had left the services after many years in the lower ranks. On looking into their backgrounds a similar story was found in almost every case. They had enlisted when they were sixteen or seventeen years old and had served for many years without promotion, carrying out the routine duties required of them. During this time they had been very much protected against the outside world. They had not had to think about where the next meal was coming from, nor when their laundry would be done, and rarely thought about buying their own clothes. The result had been that when they left the forces they were lost in the outside world. They felt as if a protective cloak had been taken away from them and because of this indulged in petty crimes. Usually these would be quite trivial things, in the hope of 'going inside' where their basic needs would once again be provided.

This was not only restricted to people from the armed services; these pathetic inadequate people are common amongst that sector of society that has led any form of institutionalised life. The old lags and the long term patients from mental hospitals also figured in this group because they had been accustomed to a form of security all their lives and they found the outside world cold, frightening and friendless when they were released.

One particular case like this which came before me has always stuck in my mind. At the time it occurred it was still possible to have milk delivered in half-pint bottles, and I was quite surprised to find that I was being asked to consider a case involving the theft of just half-a-pint of milk from a crate outside a shop. This was most unusual. The first thing I did was to ask the police officer to explain his rather extraordinary action in having the man charged over such a trivial matter. The officer looked a little sheepish and embarrassed at this request but said, 'Well madam, you see this is the ninth time that this man has been apprehended for taking milk and it was felt it was time some action was taken to prevent it continuing.'

I looked across to the pathetic man in the dock. He was clean, but his clothes were showing signs of wear and he was dejected.

'Why do you do this?' I queried.

'I haven't anywhere to go' came the reply.

'What do you mean? Haven't you any home to go to?'

'Well, yes, I've got a room where I stay.'

After further prolonged questioning and by dragging the answers out I managed to obtain the whole story. It was what I had already heard so many times. He had been discharged after serving in the army for most of his active life and with his pension had just enough to live on in this one room which he rented. But he longed for the security of a life in which there was some form of regimentation with meals at fixed times and someone to look after him. He couldn't face up to providing for himself and making his own decisions. Because of this he kept stealing the milk, not because he really needed it but because he hoped that he would eventually be put in prison, and that was the nearest he could get to being back in the army.

In a case like this the last thing any magistrate would want to do is to send the man to prison. There are enough real criminals locked away without adding unnecessarily to their numbers. In this case the man was put on probation and the social services were asked to give him a hand. But I had no doubt that in this type of case it took a great deal of help and encouragement to build up the sense of personal security comparable with the security previously enjoyed in the services.

Magistrates have to work very closely with the social services in cases in which petty crime lands people in court and where what is needed is not punishment but help. This does not mean that there is a justification of the crime or an excuse for society. But many people are really asking for help when they commit minor crimes and where possible magistrates try to provide this help through the social services and the probation service. I am only too well aware that even then some of the first offenders did become professional criminals. But the efforts were justified by the results which showed that the majority of these people did not appear in court a second time.

I always felt that the first duty of the police, the courts and the law was to protect society. The penalty meted out by the court was one that had to carry out that duty by removing the criminal from the society upon which he, or she, had been preying or by deterring them from repeating the offence. It is the community which suffers and the community which must be protected. I have always believed that the nation must always maintain a strong, well trained, well equipped, well paid police force, backed by a modern prison service. To this must be added a process of justice in which penalties can be exacted which do not enable crime to pay and in which parents are made fully responsible for the criminal acts of their children.

One of the great failures of our present system of justice is that a vandal can be found guilty of doing damage running to several hundreds of pounds but it is not normal for the court to make either the perpetrator or the parents pay for that damage. All too often restitution is only obtained if a civil action is taken by the owners of the damaged property. The same failure to make adequate restitution applies with housebreakers, bag snatchers and other thieves. The ability of the courts to make restitution orders for the victim against the criminal is still too limited and insufficient.

I acquired quite a reputation on the bench for my views on this, and overheard someone refer to me as the 'Restitution Queen'. It is a title I was proud to own because I always tried to make restitution whenever possible to people who had lost money or property. I always maintained that if an old lady was robbed of five pounds, which might be next week's rent or the price of that day's food, then giving that five pounds back to her was what she needed more than just knowing that the thug who stole it had gone to prison. I did not feel it was enough for the courts to punish the criminal whilst forgetting the real needs of the victim.

The laws in Great Britain and other countries have, in recent years, gone a long way towards helping the innocent dependants when a family wage-earner is murdered or killed in an accident. Legislation in this area was very deficient in my early days as a magistrate and I became particularly conscious of it when I encountered a case of considerable hardship arising from the death of a man due to an accident with an uninsured motorist. In this case, the widow was left with three children to bring up when her husband, on his way to mail a letter, was knocked down and killed by a reckless, uninsured driver. At that time the woman had to rely totally on the social security system, as the driver had no insurance cover to claim on, despite the fact that he was found guilty of causing the accident. As he was a 'man of straw' a civil action against him would have been a waste of money. That case became etched on my mind. I think I have always been very conscious of the needs of dependants, whether they are those of the victim or of the criminal being sent to prison, because of the financial state my mother and I found ourselves in after the *Titanic* sank.

I have previously referred to the ingratitude that I sometimes encountered in my work. It is only fair that I balance the picture, as the number of people who have thanked me for my help far exceeds those who found cause for complaint or criticism. Sometimes the thanks have come when I have least expected it, years after the events.

On one occasion I went into a small local shop which had recently changed hands and which previously I had not frequented. As I walked round selecting goods from the shelves the manageress looked at me, said 'Oh, madam!' and burst into tears. I wondered what had happened and thought she must be in some sort of trouble, so asked her what was wrong. When she had recovered and managed to control her feelings she told me that she was pleased to see me as she had never had the opportunity to thank me for the help I had given her. Apparently she was separated from her husband and he had been brought before me in court for non-payment of maintenance to her and their children. Although he had tried to justify his action by the traditional excuse of insufficient money and maintaining a new household, I had taken a strong line and insisted that he paid a regular decent amount to his first family, or risk going to prison. She told me that these payments had come just at the right time and at long last she had been able to thank me! I came away feeling that those few words of appreciation made it all worthwhile.

My work as a magistrate very quickly led me into another side of law enforcement – the prisons. I found the work here to be most enlightening as I came to know only too well the conditions I imposed upon the criminals who were convicted in front of me. I have had two responsibilities within the prisons. One was as a member of the Board of Visitors and the other as a member of the local review committee of the Parole Board.

The Board of Visitors has the responsibility of adjudicating within the prison. For that purpose I attended monthly meetings at the prison where we received reports of all the prison activities, including the work schedules, the number of prisoners, the accommodation and the behaviour of the prisoners. As part of this work we took it in turns to visit the whole of the prison on a rota and report back to the following meeting of the Board.

When I arrived at the prison for a rota visit I had to show my Home Office pass before I was admitted, and then everywhere I went doors were opened to let me through and locked firmly behind me. Security is very tight in prisons and I was conscious all the time

of being enclosed and restricted. It was impossible to disregard the
clanging of the doors and the regimented atmosphere as we walked
through the corridors although everything is done to brighten these
up by painting in a variety of light colours. In my capacity as a
member of the Board of Visitors I was free to go anywhere within
the prison; I received no instruction as to where I should or should
not go, so the decision was entirely mine. The only restriction placed
upon me was that I had to be accompanied by a prison officer, both
for my own safety and to act as a guide to parts of the prison I
didn't know. During these visits I met many of the infamous and
dangerous criminals who have been caught and punished in Great
Britain; they all seemed to arrive at the 'Scrubs' at some time during
their inprisonment.

Part of the work included dealing with disciplinary problems
and I adjudicated in cases in which prisoners were accused of
having broken the prison rules. When they were found guilty the
penalty was a loss of privileges or for the more serious offences it
would be loss of any remission they might have gained on their
original sentence. This is the only instance when I have sat in
judgement for juveniles, as the prison where I sat as a visitor was
used as an assessment or clearing centre for juvenile criminals
before they were allocated to Borstals.

I saw the education facilities within the prisons improved
greatly during the years I was visiting them. As a result, I can
truthfully say that I know of many people who have genuinely
benefited from being in prison. This was particularly so from a
training point of view, as every effort is now made to develop any
latent abilities that the prisoner may possess, in order that they
might earn a living using that ability constructively when they are
released. A large number of prisoners now have the opportunity
to take GCE accountancy and Open University examinations
while in prison. This is certainly the type of thing that should
be encouraged as much as possible as it provides them with a
qualification and a degree of self-assurance, both of which can
help them to become re-established in society.

I am frequently asked if I think prisoners are mollycoddled
these days with television, film shows and central heating. My
answer is invariably that I do not think this is the case, although
the conditions in many of our prisons have been much improved.
I am always tempted to ask the questioners if they would prefer
us to revert to the conditions of squalor which were described so
vividly by Charles Dickens.

Whilst there is some tendency to forget that the first function of prison is to constrain the criminal in order to protect the public, there is more to it than that. In my conversation with prisoners I have found that with most of them the loss of liberty is a major deterrent and a privilege they do not wish to lose again in the future. At the same time, I have considerable sympathy with prison officers who have a most difficult task to carry out and deserve more encouragement for the protection they help to give the public. It is a job that only hits the headlines when there is trouble in the prisons and goes unappreciated most of the time.

Parole Boards have an important role to play within a prison as their one main responsibility is deciding whether or not prisoners can justifiably be released on parole after completing only part of their sentences. Members took it in turns to perform the initial study and when doing so were provided with all the details of the prisoner's crimes, the prison conduct record and information about any studying that might have been carried out for professional qualifications. Having read through all the data the board member then interviewed the prisoner in an attempt to assess whether or not he or she could be released back into society at an earlier date than would normally be the case. This was, of course, a subjective assessment, although a great deal of information was studied before any recommendation was made. Fortunately, as a result of listening to many people over the years in court, some telling the truth and some telling lies, I developed an instinct for even the smallest distortion of the truth and was not inclined to recommend parole for people who I felt were trying to pull the wool over my eyes just to achieve an early release.

The full review board at that time consisted of a magistrate, an independent person, a probation officer and a senior member of the prison staff. Any final decision to recommend parole is taken by the full board which considers the report made by the person who has carried out the interview. The review board did not grant the parole, the decision for this was taken by the Parole Board at the Home Office and they did not always see eye to eye with the recommendation of the local review board.

Every prisoner can apply for parole after a set proportion of his or her sentence has been served, and that does mean every prisoner. But it does not mean that all prisoners receive parole either at the first or second application. It does mean that even murderers can be and have been paroled. I have, in fact, been a member of a review board which has recommended a murderer for parole. Although on the surface this may appear an irresponsible thing to do, it is important to remember that as capital punishment has been abolished and life sentences really only mean imprisonment for a certain number of years, the government has already taken the decision that all murderers, except the criminally insane, will eventually be considered for release back into society. The job of the review committee is only to try and decide whether that can be done at an earlier stage than the court sentence had intended. In the majority of cases I think it is unlikely that any early release for a murderer can, would or should be permitted, but there are certainly some murderers who have committed a murder for some very special reason and are no more likely than the rest of the population to commit another. Our job under these circumstances was to decide whether or not convicted murderers were going to be a further menace to society if they received parole.

At the age of seventy I had to give up my work as a magistrate on the local bench as I had reached the official age of retirement. However, for a further two years I was allowed to serve in the Crown Court and on the Board of Visitors to the prison. When I eventually had to retire completely from that sphere of work I missed the involvement with justice and the direct contact with the police and the prison officers. I didn't miss having to remind myself that the people appearing in front of the court are not typical of the population as a whole. When as a magistrate you see one petty thief after another paraded into the dock and then a group of arrogant teenage vandals, followed by a father who has beaten his wife and children unmercifully, it is possible to develop a completely jaundiced view of life. I sometimes felt that the whole world must be evil for so much crime and violence to thrive.

After a day of listening to one atrocity after another it was always a relief to get back to my small flat, to brew a cup of tea and remind myself that, for the greater part, I had for that day met the dregs of society and could now come back down to earth. For me it is now all over and I can think back to those occasions when I had to mete out the Queen's justice and decide on punishment and retribution or another chance and opportunity for someone to start again. It has been a hard bench, a demanding bench but a very satisfying job, which I learnt to do with the support and guidance of the court employees, the police and the prison staff. To them all I shall always be grateful for their consideration to this particular Justice of the Peace.

I managed to combine my employment, my work as a magistrate and my other voluntary work very well for many years to everybody's satisfaction. However, after I had been carrying out my job as a welfare officer, apparently successfully, for twenty-five years, the director who had originally appointed me died and the Sterling Engineering Company was taken over by a large holding company. It was very soon made evident to me and to the employees in the factory that this new company had very different ideas about the way in which we should operate. They certainly did not think that the type of welfare work I had been doing was necessary – as I soon found out when they gave me one month's notice.

I received a great deal of sympathy over the manner in which the whole thing was done, but there was no possibility of them reconsidering their decision or continuing with my services. Quite a number of people in similar 'non-productive' positions were asked to leave at the same time, but it came particularly hard to me. Not only had I given twenty-five years loyal service to the company but I was then sixty-three years old and unlikely to obtain a position with another company. I could, of course, have just accepted the situation and gracefully gone into retirement whilst trying to keep myself satisfied with my voluntary work.

I was very annoyed and upset at what was quite a peremptory dismissal, mainly because I did not wish to give up what was undoubtedly my true vocation. Despite my age I was still physically active and mentally capable. I felt very strongly that I still had a great deal to offer in the realms of industrial welfare and it seemed a great pity to let all that experience go to waste. It was because of this inner conviction that I quickly made up my mind to continue to work as a private consultant welfare officer.

I can assure those who also have the longing to be their own bosses that the change from being employed to becoming self-employed is not an easy one. Having worked for other people for the whole of your life it is a major decision to change the whole of your mental approach in order to put up with the difficulties and problems of working independently or privately for yourself. When you do, you are not controlled by somebody else's clock, nobody else takes the responsibility of dealing with your tax or your national insurance, you receive no sickness benefit from the state if you are ill, and you have to apply your own discipline to ensure that work is completed on time. There are many deterrents to becoming self-employed but there is also a great degree of pleasure and self-satisfaction. It always impresses me that despite the deterrents, there are still many thousands of people who are prepared to risk their capital and their time in order to be independent and their own bosses. If they are successful and become rich, good luck to them. They usually well deserve it and the nation would be much poorer without their spirit of enterprise.

Fortunately, for me, the risk was not too great a one; I knew that I could, if necessary, live on my state pension and savings. By trying to become an independent welfare officer all I really put at risk was my reputation and the possibility of being snubbed when I approached companies.

The whole thing really started because a number of the former executives from the company that had just sacked me had, over the years, branched out on their own and opened up small factories or businesses within the area in which I lived. These were mainly around Chadwell Heath, Romford and Ilford. When I sat down to compile a list I realised that there was quite a crop of these businesses, and it had not been uncommon for the various managers and owners to telephone me for advice and help for the problems which arose in their companies while I had still been employed in the engineering company full-time. I had always given this advice without thought of charging as it had been on a friendly basis and I had realised then that they were not large enough to employ their own welfare officers.

So I had happily passed on my knowledge and was now pleased I had done so. It now occurred to me that if they were not able to pay a fulltime welfare officer they might be prepared to purchase a part share in a peripatetic independent welfare officer who could either visit the company on a regular basis or be called in when required.

So I had some private note paper printed with my name and my new title – *Consultant Welfare Officer* – at the top and wrote to all the people I knew telling them of my intention. Not everyone replied, but I was totally taken aback by the enthusiasm of the response that I did receive. Most of the them were only too pleased to have the opportunity of having someone with experience to sort out the myriad of problems that arise within all companies, big and small. As one manager said, 'With only twenty employees the employment of a full-time welfare officer is out of the question. It would be too great an overhead. But on the other hand, if I am one woman short for a day because she has to sort out some rent problem I lose five per cent of my productivity. I certainly need you and can use your services.' And so I went to work again, independent at sixty-three, and wishing I had taken the step many years before.

In my new role I established a timetable for each week in which, as far as possible, I visited the various companies on a rota basis. At the same time I made sure that they all knew where they could get hold of me at any particular time and left sufficient free time to be able to deal with any emergencies that arose.

On my early visits it was a matter of being taken around to be introduced to the various employees, during which I tried to gain their confidences as quickly as possible. By the time I came round for the third or fourth visit the queries, problems and tragedies would be lined up waiting for me. Often the manager of the company would say, 'Will you have a word with Margaret, the girl at the end of the bench, she's been half an hour late for work three times this week but I cannot find out the reason why.' So I would deal with that problem first and would find that the woman had been late because she had to take her youngster to school as the grandmother who normally did it was ill. So often it was a very small thing that only needed a few words of explanation. And within these smaller companies I found that the owners and managers were very understanding and considerate to their employees and the problems they encountered.

Once one problem had been satisfactorily ironed out in each company I found the employees themselves very quickly came to me on their own to unburden their worries, and my venture into private practice thrived. My friends used to joke about it and say, 'Not bad for an old-age pensioner who nearly went down with the *Titanic!*'

In my new liberated role I found that I frequently had to deal with what I can only call 'sympathetic absenteeism'. This occurred because in most companies each employee seems to have one particular friend upon whom they lean and with whom they share their confidences. This is certainly the case with most women. The absenteeism would arise if, for instance, Mary wanted to have a tooth out and told Gladys about it. Out of sympathy and consideration Gladys would say, 'Oh dear, it will make you feel awful, I'd better come with you.'

The result would be that the following day production would drop by 10 to 15 per cent because both Gladys and Mary would be away waiting for Mary to have a tooth attended to. There would be no single answer to this type of problem. In some cases the best that could be done was to arrange for the appointment to be as late in the day as possible, and in others for someone to pick up poor Mary after the tooth had been extracted. By these means 'sympathetic absenteeism' could be reduced. But it could not be totally eliminated because of the basic considerate nature of the people who were predominantly from the East End of London and had all the qualities of the Cockneys.

Another thing that I found which cost the firms a great deal of money was the time lost by workers when they had hospital appointments. It was not uncommon for a person to apologise for not having turned up at all the previous day because they had been given a morning appointment at the local hospital and had been kept waiting so long that by the time they had been attended to it was too late to come to work. They would be upset about it themselves because it had cost them a day's earnings and the 'sympathetic absenteeism' element would also apply here. This became so serious for some of the small companies when key workers were involved that I decided I would try and use my knowledge of the local hospitals to get their co-operation in an effort to reduce this terrible waste of time. Eventually I got them to agree that if I telephoned them on behalf of a patient who was doing an important job for the company they would arrange for that patient to be seen at or close to an appointed time if I went along to the hospital with them. As a result it was possible to reduce the loss of time.

I found it quite tragic that after nearly twenty years of house building following the end of the Second World War there seemed to be no end to the continuous queue of people coming to me saying they were having difficulty in finding a house for when they got married. Many of these people were not earning enough to be able to buy a place of their own and could not expect to save up the deposit necessary in a reasonable period of time. Within the area in which I carried out my work there was virtually no private rented property available, and the only hope for many couples was to obtain one of the local council houses. I didn't profess to be able to get them a council house, but what I could do was to point out to them that some of the councils did permit engaged couples to go on the waiting lists before they were married. This in its turn often meant they got a home earlier. But I followed this advice up by acting as an intermediary between the couple and the council while they were waiting and by informing the housing officer of any changed circumstances. This meant that I saved the company which employed them time and money as they did not need time off to keep going to the council offices.

Through being a magistrate I was often presented with problems of a legal nature. Where these are particularly involved I could only advise the person to go and see a solicitor. This I always did if they wished to make a will, as too many wills have been drawn up incorrectly by amateurs usually leading to the intended beneficiaries losing out completely. But I had instances of women appearing in front of me sporting black eyes and wanting to know what steps they had to take to obtain legal separations from their husbands. Another frequent enquiry came from teenagers wanting guidance on contraception. If I was unable to provide the advice myself I could normally tell them the right places to go in order to obtain the information they needed. In fact, most of the time I found that my work as a consultant welfare officer necessitated being a walking fount of information waiting to be tapped by the various employees.

The reward in all this was to see the change on their faces which lit up when they realised that there was an answer to their problems and that someone was interested and did care.

One sidelight that has come out of all this work was that it gave me the opportunity to see many different sides of British industry. I have watched people working in drawing offices, seen machine guns being made, shirts, skirts and dresses being cut and sewn, and electric coils being wound. I can confidently say that the British worker is not lazy, nor is he or she incompetent. Most of the people I have met are hard-working individuals who wish to be paid a reasonable wage for their job in order to provide a good standard of living for their families. They, do not wish to strike and they do wish to be able to get on with their jobs. In the smaller companies, those with which I have been associated, labour relations were good and I like to think that I helped to contribute something to maintain that state of affairs.

Working for myself gave me opportunities and a freedom I had never previously imagined possible. I enjoyed my work of meeting and helping people so much that I continued to do it as long as I was able to and my services were required.

In these days of expanding social services it has become common to criticise the voluntary worker as a 'do-gooder'. So may I say that as a well labelled 'do-gooder' that it is not the doing good which simply motivates those of us involved in any form of voluntary service. The real motivation is very much more involved and difficult to define. But in most cases it comes down to a genuine desire to participate in and to be of service to the community.

At a time of mass production and demanding commuting to and from work, there is no doubt that many people are failing to obtain true personal satisfaction within their employment. They find in the realms of voluntary service a greater freedom of opportunity to express themselves and to contribute more meaningfully to the world around them. In so doing they become more complete and more satisfied with their lives.

I find that the critics of voluntary service are all too often those who are prepared to accept such services when they require them but deride them with cynicism and scepticism when they see others helping and being helped. Frequently people say, 'You only do it for what you can get out of it.'

By that they usually imply that there is some financial rake-off for assisting Guide Dogs for the Blind, or some graft to be made from running jumble sales for Oxfam. More often it is a weak excuse in order that they can justify not helping because they are above such hypothetical graft. In one sense they are correct. Doing any form of voluntary work does have a reward to it. That reward is the personal satisfaction of doing something worthwhile – it is the smile of gratitude on the face of a blind person receiving their first guide dog – it is the relief of a whole family when they learn that they are going to get a house of their own – it is the tears in the eyes of a child opening the wrappings of an unexpected Christmas present.

In these days of government hand-outs and egalitarianism the 'do-gooder' has been criticised, taken for granted and squeezed out, but despite this still has a major part to play in maintaining a stable fabric to the disintegrating society in which we live. Who would bear the cost of teaching first aid in the absence of the Red Cross Society and the St John's Ambulance Brigade? Not the state, with the cost of the Health Service already escalating every year! Which government department can make a better job of raising money for the under-developed nations and the poor of the world than the Save the Children Fund or Oxfam?
Make no mistake about it, the moral and spiritual standing of any nation is much reduced and the people lacking in compassion if voluntary help is stopped or dries up.

Those people who seek to exclude volunteers from working in hospitals and who place the sole responsibility for social care upon the state show an appalling lack of understanding of human need. The volunteer is less likely to have to meet a time schedule and can often give that extra care or travel that second mile, that many a paid official is unable or unwilling to do. It should always be remembered that the voluntary worker is undertaking a task because he or she wishes to do it and as a result their enthusiasm alone is sufficient to overcome enormous difficulties.

I do not think I can adequately explain why I was so active in voluntary work, except to say that there is something deep inside me which encouraged me, led me and drove me on. It was not just something to do but rather something that had to be done. I can best explain it by telling of the only time I ever had my fortune told.

I was on holiday in Wales in 1955 and was standing in the sunshine on the Great Orme at Landudno when a fairly nondescript elderly woman approached me. Just by looking at me she told me I was an Aquarian and then asked for my date of birth. There then followed the most accurate bit of astrology I have ever heard. Having never met me before and knowing nothing about me she proceeded to describe my attitude to voluntary work and my involvement in society as a whole. The analysis she gave was so precise as to be uncanny. She said:

You are the type of person who appears to thrive on responsibility and are destined to spend a great deal of time getting other people out of trouble. You are the exception to the rule if you haven't someone dependant upon you, and in all probability the important affairs in your life will be very much tied up with relatives and the family circle. You have inherited a very strong sense of duty, and if you haven't family duties of your own you will associate yourself with welfare work of some kind. At heart you are a humanitarian, and can be extraordinarily sympathetic towards those even of whom you do not approve. In friendships you are intensely loyal and sincere, but you are not the type of person to fall in love easily. There is a tremendous amount of clear judgement and common sense about you. Your taste in most things is reliable, and it is more than likely that you possess a highly developed artistic instinct and are very musical. You are capable of a lot of tenacity once you get going, but you definitely belong to the group of people who like to take their time and refuse to come to important decisions without plenty of consideration. The thrills of life do not appeal to you as strongly as some people, and your aims lean more towards security than sensationalism.

Having been laid bare like that made me wonder if my motives and reasons for being so deeply involved in everything were equally transparent to other people. After all, it is not common for total strangers to approach people and proceed to put astrology or character analysis to work. Whatever it was, that woman captured my attitudes admirably, because most of the work, paid and voluntary, with which I have been involved has concerned people, their problems, difficulties and worries in some form or another. In many instances, my involvement started by accident or casually – invariably it finished up in my being involved very deeply.

My work for the National Savings Movement was a case in point. I had never expected or intended that my involvement would extend as far as it did. The initial fund raising during the war finally led to an active role for over twenty years. In my capacity as chairman for the Dagenham area, I had to keep an eye on all the factory and local National Savings groups in the area, as well as represent their views at the national committee. I felt that was certainly a job worth doing and was sorry when eventually I had to give it up. I was greatly honoured when I was presented with a plaque by the Mayor at the Dagenham Civic Centre recording my service to the movement. During those years I was actively involved in helping to raise many thousands of pounds for National Savings by the combined efforts of all those small groups of people who are so often forgotten when appreciation is being expressed.

My involvement in party politics continued after the Second World War. Like the rest of the Conservative Party our organisation in the Romford division had been disbanded for the duration of the war. Whilst this was undoubtedly the correct decision at the time, it was a major disadvantage when the 1945 General Election came upon us as the Labour Party had maintained their organisation all the time.

In fact, the Conservative Party campaign for the 1945 election for the new Dagenham constituency was actually run from my flat as we had no other headquarters. Our candidate on that occasion was Squadron Leader A. E. (Teddy) Cooper, fresh from fighting in the war. He failed to win against the enormous socialist landslide but went on to become the Conservative Member of Parliament for the adjacent constituency of Ilford South in 1950.

It was at this time that I became chairman of the local Conservative Party and spent the next few years helping to rebuild the organisation in what was one of the strongest socialist seats in Great Britain. This was a major spare time occupation until 1949 when I had to have an operation on my left leg. My leg was injured during the war when I slipped while running for shelter in the Civic Centre when there was an air raid. It had not been broken, and appeared to have recovered from the tumble after a short time. But in 1949 an X-ray showed that the knee joint had worn my kneecap paper-thin and that had to be removed before it broke up. Shortly after the operation, just when I thought I was back to normal, I slipped again – this time I broke all the tendons in that part of my leg.

Since then I have had to walk slowly, keeping my leg as straight as possible and climbing stairs can be a rather laborious process. Fortunately, I am rarely in pain from it unless I knock it, and it is more of a nuisance than anything else. It did however put a stop to my driving as I could no longer depress a clutch pedal and meant I was unable to lead canvassing teams or go out delivering leaflets. For quite a time I felt a bit like a lame duck so I passed the chairmanship over to another capable person and was elevated to the less active position of president.

Despite this loss in physical activity, my interest in politics, local and national, has not waned. Although Dagenham has never been a hot bed of Conservatism, it has been a very useful political nursery. Norman St John Stevas, who was later to become a government minister, cut his political teeth by fighting Dagenham in 1951, and one of our own Young Conservative chairmen went on to contest two other parliamentary seats.

I did not, however, see politics as the only way to help people. Politicians who think that, or who believe that the state machinery has all the answers, are deluding themselves. As far as I am concerned, it is people that count and the important thing is to find some genuine way in which those in need can be assisted – whether through politics, social services, the local council, the church or by voluntary organisations.

It comes as quite a surprise to many people when they find that I was greatly involved with the Family Planning Association for many years. For some reason they assume that an elderly spinster could not, or should not, be interested in such personal and intimate matters. After all, what could I possibly know about such things? The fact of the matter is that after more than thirty-five years as a welfare officer there are few personal, private or intimate details that could shock me; and many of the things I have seen and heard would make most people's hair curl.

I strongly believe that family planning is not only a private matter, but also a national and international problem. It should always be emphasised that it is not just a matter of birth control but of planning as well as possible to have a family in an organised manner in order to provide adequately for each additional child as it arrives. And whilst I greatly respect the view of those people who do not hold with artificial birth control, I do not agree with them and feel they are failing to face up to the social, political and population problems which arise in those countries in which family planning is not adequately carried out.

My own work in this field started in the late 1950s. Until that time there had been no Family Planning Association in Dagenham and the national body of the FPA decided to try and get one off the ground. I was approached, in my capacity as a magistrate, along with local ministers, church workers, doctors and social workers, in order to find out if there was sufficient support to form a local group. After meeting and agreeing to go ahead we were able to obtain facilities for the work in a nearby clinic.

As much as possible of the work was carried out on a voluntary basis, lay workers were recruited locally where possible. The doctors and nurses were the only people paid for their services in those early days. We started by providing the service on one evening per week and very quickly had to extend it to a second evening. We proved that a demand for the service certainly did exist and it has continued to exist ever since. It grew to such an extent that we were later provided with much more extensive facilities in a modem clinic and were open most evenings of the week.

I remained involved with this work until it was taken over by the Area Health Authority in 1976 as part of the Ministry of Health, when I was informed that my services were no longer required because of my age!

I saw many changes and developments in family planning during my voluntary work for the FPA, but I always had grave reservations about the increased use of vasectomy. Contrary to many publications, it is not always as painless and as uncomplicated as frequently presented. Although its main virtue is that it is quick, easy and relatively cheap to carry out. Once it is done and the man is sterile it is possible for the husband and wife to have a full physical relationship without recourse to physical or chemical barriers, or the need for the wife to take a cycle of drugs. It means that sexual intercourse can be considered in a perfectly natural context without advance planning.

The main disadvantage as I see it is that the operation is frequently irreversible. This is not important in the majority of cases. But I have met a man whose wife and children were killed in an accident and he was very upset at being unable to have another family. This is, perhaps, a morbid way of looking at it. However, I would not advise any man to have a vasectomy under the age of forty or unless he is quite certain his family is complete. In any case, no husband should have the operation unless his wife agrees, and only then if they are both fully aware of all the consequences.

Despite my reservations, I do know of many married couples who are very happy and who enjoy improved sexual relationships following successful vasectomies. I am fully convinced that sensible, responsible family planning has much to commend it and am pleased to have assisted husbands and wives in establishing and maintaining happy marriages.

Voluntary work in the community does not always mean a deep involvement such as that which I enjoyed with the National Savings Movement and the FPA. Ever since I played with that French Bulldog on the *Titanic* I have been fond of dogs and regularly attend the Crufts Dog Show. I had not, however, fully appreciated the value of a dog serving in a greater role than just as a companion or pet until I became the welfare officer in the engineering factory. Two of the employees at the factory were totally blind and every day I saw the immense value of the guide dogs in helping these two people to lead very full lives and to carry out a full day's work. The training that the dogs undergo is lengthy and, of course, expensive, but there is no doubt that it is worth it for the increased confidence and mobility of those blind people who have guide-dogs.

Because of this firsthand experience we organised collections periodically in the factory to help finance other dogs, and even now I try to raise money in various small ways in order to help the movement along. It is just a small participation, but one that is well worthwhile if it assists other people to get around more easily.

One of the most impressive organisations with which I came into contact during my welfare work was Dr Barnado's (now usually just referred to as Barnados).

Although I was not a voluntary worker for it myself, it is a perfect example of how well organised volunteers can provide money and facilities to cater for the people in need around them.

The main centre of Dr Barnardo's at Barkingside is only a short distance from my flat and on one occasion I needed to ask for their help, which was given with no hesitation. I had been presented with a problem of a family of five children all under the age of eleven years, with a father dying of cancer and a mother who was mentally unstable. The children, who had been brought up for months on a diet consisting virtually only of milk, were unruly, sullen and bad mannered. Despite the problems, or because of them, Dr Barnardo's took those children into their family units, kept them together and brought them up. When I learnt that the first action of one of the children on seeing a table spread for tea was to pull the tablecloth with the knives, forks, plates, jam and bread on to the floor, I knew it was not going to be an easy task. But the people at Dr Barnardo's did a marvellous job and those children grew up and became responsible, successful adults. All because of one man who cared enough to start the organisation and thanks to the voluntary workers who still care enough to raise the money.

Over the years I have served on many different bodies and committees, sometimes representing the magisterial bench, or family planning or in some other capacity. I have been a school manager and school governor, and have served on hospital committees and during these years have met many different people serving in the same capacities. There have been many occasions when I have disagreed with my colleagues and they with me, but I am convinced that without our combined voluntary efforts on behalf of the community there would be fewer safeguards for the protection of us all. The voluntary worker needs to be encouraged if only to counterbalance the increasing domination of the state.

One morning towards the end of 1973 I received one of the biggest shocks of my life. I opened one of the many official envelopes which arrived by almost every post. But this was something different from usual – I read that the Queen wished to bestow upon me the honour of Membership of the Most Noble Order of the British Empire. I was being asked if I would accept an MBE for my public and political services. Would I accept? I was almost delirious. Who had suggested me for the honour? I didn't know. But I couldn't ask and couldn't tell anyone until the Honours List was published on 1 January 1974.

It was incredible; I had never ever thought that the work I did so willingly and from which I derived so much satisfaction and pleasure would receive such recognition. After the Honours List was published I was deluged with congratulations from hundreds of friends from all over the country, but it was sometime before the wife of one particular friend let slip that her husband had written to the Prime Minister suggesting I deserved to be honoured.

To receive the MBE I attended an investiture at Buckingham Palace at which the Duke of Kent was presenting the various honours. It had been intended that the presentations would be made by the Queen herself, but that day she had to withdraw as she was due to meet the newly elected Prime Minister, Harold Wilson, to discuss the composition of his proposed Cabinet. The presentation took place during the industrial crisis of 1974 when Britain was in the middle of a miners' strike and power cuts, so the Palace was cold and only partially lit. Despite this, the organisation was impeccable.

All those being presented were allowed to take two guests who had seats to watch the proceedings in the investiture hall. I was taken to join the long queue of people waiting to receive awards for valour, long service or voluntary work. The two men in front of me were both sailors being presented with medals for bravery on board ship, but all I could get them to tell me was that one of them had been badly burned in a fire.

While we waited, an official pinned a hook to the left side of our coats and carefully checked that we were in the correct order. Then, as the queue gradually moved forward, we reached the door to the hall. As we each came to the head of the line we were stopped and told to wait until the person in front had been presented, then instructed to take so many steps along the red carpet into the hall to stand in front of the Duke. After all the waiting I was terribly nervous; then my name was read out – Miss Eva M. Hart, MBE – and despite my bad leg I managed to walk steadily, without tripping, to have the medal placed on the hook on my coat.

I treasure that award and recognise it as a real honour. It still surprises me that anyone should feel I deserve it, but I am grateful and pleased to have it. Whatever criticisms may have been made about the Honours List, it does provide the opportunity to give some recognition in a tangible form to ordinary citizens to whom a purely financial payment would be inappropriate.

10

THE SHIP THAT STILL LIVES ON

Once again the world's largest, most expensive and glamorous liner was dying. We had seen her slowly filling with water after hitting the iceberg, the lifeboats had all rowed away from the ship; and now, gracefully, almost majestically, but still horribly, she stood almost vertically in the water with her stem pointing to the cold Atlantic sky. I couldn't look any longer, I shut my eyes and turned away, while around me there was a total silence as the ship then slid smoothly and quietly below the waves.

Despite having seen the film *A Night to Remember* several times since attending the Premiere at the Odeon Theatre in London's Leicester Square on 3 July 1958, I have never been able to bring myself to look at the part where the ship actually sinks. The first time I saw the film it brought back all my nightmares for some time afterwards and I just cannot face seeing the ship sinking again. The film itself was so realistic and so well produced that, from my own experiences, I was unable to fault anything about it.

Before the film was made I had met Walter Lord, the author of the book upon which the film is based. He had written to and interviewed as many of the survivors of the disaster as possible in an effort to make his book as historically correct as possible. This very high standard was maintained by the producer of the film, William MacQuitty, who went to great lengths to achieve authenticity and historical accuracy. I have always been impressed by the very high standards achieved by everyone connected with the film. Any help

I could give was rather limited as I could not go into any great technical detail about the ship and only knew about that part of the ship in which I had been free to roam and play for those five days. Some of the other survivors had been of considerable assistance in being able to state quite clearly where various objects had been placed and the order in which the lifeboats had been lowered down the sides of the ship. All the information provided had been put together and used in the 48 feet model which had been built for the filming. This was the centre of attraction in the theatre foyer, displayed for all to see at the Premiere.

Edith Russell, who had been one of the first class passengers, was able to give the film makers all the details about the musical box made to look like a pig which she had carried with her into the lifeboat and which she used to entertain the children during the cold night. I met Miss Russell, whom I sometimes visited in her London flat, and about a dozen other survivors at a reunion arranged during the film Premiere. That was the biggest reunion of survivors from the *Titanic* that there has been in Britain. Since then many, including Edith Russell, have died and only a handful now remain to tell the tale. Of course, some of the younger survivors who were only babies at the time have no memories of the disaster and were unable to give any help to the film makers.

The film distributors turned the premiere into a major event and the guests that evening included the Rt Hon Selwyn Lloyd, at that time British Foreign Secretary, and the then President of the Board of Trade, Sir David Eccles, as well as many other titled people and famous actors and actresses. In the company of the other *Titanic* survivors I was photographed for the national and local newspapers wearing my silver and blue brocade gown with dark blue sandals and a fox fur.

It was at the reunion, after seeing the film, that we all had the opportunity to meet Kenneth More, the star of the film who played the role of Second Officer Charles Lightoller. His was a marvellous bit of acting. Before I saw the film I had felt there would be a great danger that Kenneth More's personality might dominate the film. But the production was very well done and throughout the film all we could think about was the *Titanic* as the centre-piece of that long drawn-out agony. I was delighted to get both Kenneth More and James Cairney to autograph my copy of Walter Lord's book. I also took the opportunity to persuade Lawrence Beesley, one of the other survivors, to autograph a reprint of his book *The Loss of the Titanic*.

Several other films have also been made about the *Titanic* and it has formed the basis of a number of fictional scripts. Twentieth Century Fox had made an earlier version of the tragedy, simply called *Titanic,* in 1953, starring Clifton Webb, Barbara Stanwyck and Robert Wagner. A German film of the disaster also exists, but *A Night to Remember* is by far the most exact and realistic presentation of the tragedy that I have ever seen.

Even after all these years the *Titanic* pops up in the most unexpected places, almost as if I am not permitted to push it aside for very long. I may pick up a novel and find I am reading a story involving exchanges of identity introduced by means of confusion at the time of the sinking of the liner – a technique beautifully used by John Dickson Carr in *The Crooked Hinge,* or I read that someone has invented (!) a game called *Titanic* – not something I wish to play! It was certainly no party game for those who endured the real thing. It also figures in television plays quite unexpectedly and a major part of the story in the famous television series *Upstairs, Downstairs* revolved around the loss of life on the *Titanic.* And, regrettably, I sometimes read an obituary of another survivor as our numbers steadily decrease. But through it all the ghost of the ship has a quite incredible permanence.

By the time I was interviewed during the making of *A Night to Remember* I had managed to conquer my general apprehension and fear of talking about the disaster. This had actually occurred more by accident than by design. After many years of choosing not to talk about it, I reached my fortieth year, shortly after the Second World War, with my feelings still mainly bottled up inside me. At this time I was asked casually by a friend if I would go with her to some small meeting. While I was there the subject of the *Titanic* came up and I was asked to give a few minutes talk about what I had seen of the disaster. I tried to say no, but as the meeting had been a little lifeless I felt an obligation to add some interest to the proceedings. The people who heard me speak at that meeting must have been quite impressed by what I had to say because they went home and told a lot of their friends and relations that I had survived the sinking of the *Titanic*. Almost immediately, and as a result of local press reports, I started receiving regular requests to visit historical societies, Women's Institutes and civic clubs to tell the story over and over again.

Somehow, the BBC came to learn about me, probably from one of the local press reports after one of my talks, and asked me to appear on a television panel game. This seemed unusual at the time. I asked myself whatever form of panel game could involve either me or the *Titanic*. Eventually, I was told what it was all about and was required to turn up at the studios in London to be one half of the subject in a game called *Find the Link.* The four people forming the panel were required to establish the common feature connecting two people presented to them. On this occasion the panel included Moira Lister and Kenneth Home and they had all become very proficient at establishing the common denominator between subjects.

Question followed question and the team started to look rather bewildered; I thought we were going to get away with it, but on the very last question, almost in desperation, or by telepathy, one of the team said 'the *Titanic'* and we had lost. My colleague with whom I was linked was an old sailor who had travelled from Southampton for the show. I think he was as disappointed as me that we had failed to win. But it showed us both how vividly the memory of the *Titanic* still remained. That appearance in its turn led to a number of other television and radio appearances. But that panel game is really the only broadcast with a light-hearted side that I have made. Most of the other interviews and programmes have been concerned with the more serious aspects of events leading up to and following the tragedy.

What has always surprised me has been the way in which the sinking of so many other ships seem to take second place to the *Titanic*. Even the horror of the attack on the *Lusitania,* which greatly influenced the attitude of the USA in the First World War, does not get as regularly resurrected, or in the same way as the pride of the White Star Line. Perhaps it is because the *Titanic* heralded the end of an era of opulence and class distinction and was at the same time the epitome of man's arrogance and self-satisfaction. Whatever it was, the *Titanic* still lives on as a lesson to everyone and a landmark in the maritime history of the world.

Some years ago, in the USA, a group of people formed the *Titanic* Enthusiasts of America, now known as the *Titanic* Historical Society, for the purpose of investigating and perpetuating the memory of the liners *Olympic, Titanic* and *Britannic.* Known survivors of the *Titanic* disaster like myself have been given honorary membership of the Society and regularly receive their magazine *The Titanic Commutator.* Even after all these years, with many articles and books having been published, this organisation is still able to uncover fresh information about the three sister ships. Its historical role certainly received great impetus from the discovery of the wreckage in September 1985.

There is always a special amount of interest in the *Titanic* on each additional 10th anniversary and since the 40th anniversary in 1952, I had this regular peak of requests for radio, television and newspaper interviews. One reason I think I have been contacted so regularly is because I was not only still living in the Greater London area but at the time was still reasonably mobile and lucid despite my advancing years. Now that the 80th anniversary has been and gone, I doubt that there will be many survivors left by the time the 90th anniversary comes round in the year 2002. Although there is every likelihood that public interest in the *Titanic* will continue, as it shows no sign of diminishing with time.

I found that people who did not know me always tended to imagine me as some fragile, doddering old lady ready to expire with the next puff of wind. When preparing this biography I had not reached that stage entirely, even if I am not as active and as mobile as I was when I was eighty. But it did account for one gentleman's actions some years ago when he invited me to speak at a dinner in a town 80 miles from London. He telephoned me almost nightly during the week prior to the dinner enquiring about my health and welfare, asking me if I knew which trains to catch and where to change. He showed concern and consideration to a totally unexpected degree. Then when I eventually arrived he couldn't believe that I was his speaker. He told me that he was quite sure that, having survived the *Titanic* disaster, I would probably be unable to walk and need help in getting to the dinner.

In many ways it is a little dismaying the way in which many people who should know better tend to write you off as being infirm and incapable of anything just because you are nearly *ninety*. We all have to get old and inevitably that brings a deterioration in one's faculties. But many old fogeys like me are still capable of doing active work, of completing difficult crossword puzzles and of holding erudite conversations.

One great benefit from accepting speaking engagements to talk about my experiences on the *Titanic* has been that it has led to me travelling a great deal in my own country and occasionally abroad. I have been interviewed in countries as far apart as Canada and Australia, as well as in France, Germany and the USA.

One of the most exhausting broadcasts I took part in was in 1969 for Télévision Francais. I was flown to Paris just for the programme to sit with (French) shipping experts able to discuss various aspects of the ship and the disaster. Altogether, the show lasted for 3 ½ hours. It included part of the German film about the sinking of the *Titanic,* which was the first time most of us had seen it. The programme also included interviews and discussions with each person present. The French certainly went to considerable pains over the presentation and I was told that it was considered a very successful broadcast. But it was a most demanding evening for effort and concentration by the participants.

I think one of the most fascinating broadcasts I made was in 1977 when the Canadian Broadcasting Company had me flown over to Winnipeg to take part in a television series called *Beyond Reason.* I thought then how incredible it was that I should be going as a survivor of the *Titanic* to the very city that my father would have been instrumental in constructing but for that very same disaster. In fact, the television programme turned out to be something far different from anything else I had ever been involved with.

The series concerned extra-sensory perception (more commonly known as ESP) with three sensitives, an astrologer, a psychometrist and a medium specialising in impressions obtained from handwriting. Their role was to try and establish individually what was special or particular about the human subjects presented before them.

Every precaution was taken before the recording session to ensure that none of those involved either met the sensitives or were known to be in Winnipeg. We were all kept secretly at separate hotels around the city before being driven straight to the studio where we were shut in a caravan until it was our turn to meet the experts.

Details of my birthday had been given to the astrologer twenty-four hours prior to the show but for the other two I had to provide a personal object, a ring I always wear for the psychometrist and a specimen of handwriting for the third medium.

For the purposes of the production they were not allowed to see me, nor me to see them, although separate cameras were recording each one of us. The sensitives were then allowed a set period of time to establish what was important about me, employing their own realm of ESP for that purpose. I was only allowed to acknowledge if they were right or wrong by answering 'yes' or 'no' as appropriate. Although none of them said that I had survived a major tragedy at sea they were all incredibly accurate in many other ways about my life and my travels. Had a little more time been allocated I am certain that at least one of them would have come up with the main answer.

They were even more accurate with the several famous people who were on the programme, including Buzz Aldrin the astronaut, and June Allyson the film star. I think we all came away feeling that the three experts seemed to have some very special gifts and that we had been privileged to see ESP at work. I must admit that I would have liked to have seen the whole series when it was transmitted in order to judge how accurate they had been with all the people studied.

I encountered many different audiences in my travels but found that the reaction of teenagers to me was one of almost total amazement. They looked at me with open-mouthed wonder in their eyes. To them I was literally a page out of the history book. It's almost as if they take the view that I really had no right to be alive in the world at the same time as them. Not that they are ever rude about it, but I saw them frantically calculating how old I must be if I was seven years old at the time the ship sank. And they blinked with shock when they realised I was as old as their great-grandparents. My story does help history come alive a little to people of that particular age group.

One thing that does annoy me is the way in which so many of the reports and feature writers for newspapers and magazines have managed to distort various aspects of the accident and of my own story in their articles. This is often due to their failure to check the details properly despite the great amount of source material available. One reporter in Australia claimed that when the *Titanic* sank it went down leaving a great void and sucked down everything with it. But this is certainly not what I said or remember, and is contrary to all the detailed reports that were made after the tragedy. At least one edition of *Encyclopaedia Britannica* stated that the *Carpathia* arrived twenty minutes after the *Titanic* disappeared below the water. If only it had, then many of those in the water would have stood a better chance of being saved. Another major publication that has sold very widely has given the year of the disaster as 1911 instead of 1912. Many different figures are quoted and misquoted for the number of people who survived and died. Probably we will never know the true figures after all this time, but those calculated by the British inquiry are almost certainly the most accurate and are generally accepted by those who have studied the details of events before and after the accident.

In an effort to counteract some of the distortions that have been made, I have always been pleased to co-operate with anyone seeking the truth as I know it. Undoubtedly, the most well researched book about the ship and the disaster is *The Maiden Voyage.* The author of this book, Geoffrey Marcus, came to see me in my flat after the book was published and told me that to ensure authenticity he had been waiting on the doorstep of the Public Records Office at Kew, near London, the day the official records were released for public viewing. He studied a wealth of documents not previously available and in his writing did not hesitate to criticise what he considered was the inactivity of the *Californian,* which he felt could have done so much more to reduce the loss of life.

It was after *The Maiden Voyage* was published in 1969 that the Canadian Broadcasting Corporation produced a special programme about the *Titanic* that was eventually put on to a gramophone record. It was sold in a very attractive folder with many illustrations of the ship and of some of the survivors, including Edith Russell and myself, who had been interviewed for the programme. Part of the record deals with the criticism of the apparent inaction of the *Californian* in not going immediately to the aid of the stricken liner and the suggestion is made that other ships in the vicinity were in better positions to help.

The argument put forward was that the *Californian* was about twenty miles from the *Titanic* and probably between the two was the Norwegian sealer *Samson.* That may well be correct. But I do know that from the lifeboats we could see a ship all the while we were on the water. Had it been the *Samson* it would have been moving away and soon lost to sight. The lookouts on the *Californian* saw rockets that could only have been distress signals, but instead of waking up the wireless operator they just tried hand-signalling with a Morse lamp. Beyond that, no action was taken – a call for help at sea in the middle of a field of icebergs was ignored by the *Californian* and possibly by others! There is certainly no doubt that the *Californian* was in the area as it was contacted early the following morning by the *Carpathia* and asked to search the surrounding sea for debris and bodies. The case put forward on the CBC record has never sounded totally plausible to me. The whole matter about the role of the *Californian* and Captain Stanley Lord has been discussed and dissected many times over the years. I have followed with great interest the attempts of the Lord family to clear the family name of the ignominy with which it has been associated following the disaster and the various inquiries. The whole matter was further aired in the United Kingdom by the Marine Accident Investigation Branch of the Ministry of Transport in 1990. A reappraisal of the evidence relating to the location of the *Californian* and Captain

Lord's actions was initiated by the MAIB and a further report released in April 1992. Whilst this report stated that the *Californian* was probably 17 to 20 miles away from the *Titanic,* it also emphasised that the distress rockets released by the *Titanic* were seen by crew on the *Californian* and no appropriate action was taken, although it would not have been possible for the *Californian* to have reached the *Titanic* before it sank. The whole matter has been very well dealt with in considerable depth by Leslie Reade and Edward De Groot in *The Ship That Stood Still,* and my own views have not changed over the years.

Shortly after obtaining a copy of the CBC record, I was asked if I would mind recording a tape for use in another recording called *The Sinking of the Titanic.* I agreed to the request and in due course was visited by a young man replete with the necessary recording equipment who told me my story would be used in a musical representation of the disaster. Some months after the taping session I was sent a copy of the record as I had been promised. It had been published by a relatively unknown company and I put it on my record player and anxiously sat down to hear how my contribution had been incorporated.

I can only say that after many years of singing choral and operatic works, of playing the piano and teaching music, it can only be described as being out of this world. I don't know which world it is in, but it certainly isn't mine and in no way conjures up memories of the *Titanic* even if it does give me nightmares of a different type. My small contribution came out as a remote, lost voice submerged by a dismal dirge of noise – with little of what I said being distinguishable. It could, in fact, have been someone reciting Kubla Khan and nobody would know the difference. I am afraid this in no way assisted in developing my appetite for modern music, nor did it encourage me to give future interviews without having a clear idea of how the information would be used.

The sound of that record certainly did not please me, but I was even more annoyed when I saw a vodka advertisement in which a poorly clad woman was being saved at sea by a lifebelt bearing the name RMS *Titanic.* To say it was in bad taste is expressing my feelings mildly. I immediately complained to the British Advertising Standards Authority and told them I deplored the abuse of the *Titanic* disaster in this way. I was not the only person to object and the advertisement was quickly withdrawn. But I still wonder what type of distorted mind was needed to use such a tragic disaster for a sales promotion! Despite that, attempts are still made to use the *Titanic* in various ways to promote sales of things like insurance by at least some form of innuendo.

I have received a large number of letters from all over the world asking me details of my life, and even for mementoes. Unfortunately, very few enclose any form of return postage, but I always tried to reply to as many as possible, especially to those from children. The Royal Mail never failed to impress me with its ability to get letters to me when they are addressed in the vaguest ways.

One of the best was sent to me from the USA as:

Miss Eva Hart MBE,
Retired Welfare Officer & Justice of the Peace &
Titanic Survivor,
living near London and 87 years old,
Do Your Best Post Office,
England.

Another from Sweden was rather oddly mailed to:

Miss Eva Hart,
The Church in Chadwell Heath,
Chadwell Heath, Essex,
United Kingdom.

And even less informative was:

Miss E. Hart,
Road number or house name unknown,
Romford, Essex.

I have visions of a big sign in the local sorting offices telling the postmen 'Anything for EVA HART send to Chadwell Heath!'

For a number of years I was approached by people who considered that it would be worth spending a great deal of money in an effort to raise the *Titanic* from its watery grave 12,000 feet down at the bottom of the Atlantic, then believed to be at latitude 41 ° 46'N and longitude 50° 14'W. This was by no means a new idea and seems to be revived every few years as new techniques are developed that might be capable of creating the buoyancy necessary to refloat the ship.

After the Second World War, the salvage vessel *Help* was seen taking soundings in the disaster area and was believed to be trying to locate the wreck. After that it was suggested that the refloating could be achieved by packing the hull with nylon bags which would then be pumped full of oil. No consideration was apparently given to the potential pollution dangers if the bags leaked or burst. An alternative idea was to strap several hundreds of large plastic containers around the wreck and to electrolyse the water inside to produce the gases hydrogen and oxygen in order to create sufficient buoyancy. As it has been estimated that the dead weight of the hulk is now over 85,000 tonnes due to the accumulated deposit of silt, raising the ship from the depths would create enormous problems.

At a depth of 2,000 fathoms the pressure to be overcome is three-quarters of a million pounds per square foot. However, the discovery of the wreck shows that the ship suffered more than just the direct damage from striking the iceberg. I have always told the audiences to whom I recounted those tragic events that I was convinced that the *Titanic* broke in half before sinking, as many other witnesses also reported; and severe damage was also heard to occur as the boilers broke from their mountings and slid through the ship. This view was clearly vindicated when the wreck was found by Bob Ballard's exploration team in 1985.

The reason for all this interest in possible salvage is because it has been claimed that when the ship sank, it not only took with it 1,502 lives but also about £100 million in money and stocks and shares and £1 ½ million worth of jewellery. This is a distortion; the assets of the people who died were considered to be £100 million, but they did not necessarily have those assets on board with them. Despite official denials about the wealth, the syndicates proposing to raise the *Titanic* base the financial justification for the exercise on the rumour that she was carrying bullion in her hold during that fateful maiden voyage.

However accurate these figures may be, I personally would wish to have no part nor to lend any support to proposals to raise what is left of the *Titanic*. To do such a thing now would desecrate the grave of the many unfortunate passengers and crew still entombed inside the hulk of that once proud ship. I can see very little to be gained from a vast expense on a corroded piece of metal which could never be restored and would only be fit for use as scrap metal. Whatever the validity of the valuation put upon the wealth on board, it is doubtful if much of that which was known to be there still exists. It has been clearly established that many of the passengers did manage to obtain their personal jewels from the pursers before the ship sank. In these instances the jewels would have gone with the survivors or have been scattered with the victims. Most of the other wealth was in the form of paper money, bearer bonds and share certificates and these would hardly have lasted through more than eighty years submersion in the depths of the ocean.

I must admit that when I first heard that *Titanic* had been found by Bob Ballard's underwater exploration group in 1985 I was filled with great trepidation, as I imagined that this could mean hordes of treasure seekers trying to dredge any objects they could from the site. But Dr Ballard has made it clear that has never been his intention and he is as anxious as I am that the actual ship and its remains should be left untouched. I have been fortunate enough to meet Dr Ballard on several occasions and have appeared on television with him. I have found him a most pleasant, relaxed and reassuring person and was delighted when he invited me to the publication of his book *The Discovery of the Titanic* at London's Savoy Hotel in September 1987. Needless to say, when I look at my copy of that beautiful book it brings back all my memories of the events that occurred.

I can still think of no justifiable reason for raising the *Titanic* and would like to see Canada extend her territorial waters far enough to include the area in which the ship is known to lie in order that it can be declared sacrosanct from fortune hunters, scavengers and ghouls. It has not been possible to keep predators at bay for very long, especially as there is a very ready market for anything associated with the *Titanic.* It is appalling to know that my father's grave is now being desecrated by people anxious to dredge up and sell anything they can from the wreckage area. But to the French bounty hunters there appears to be nothing sacrosanct about a foreign graveyard.

Let the *Titanic* rest in peace as a memorial to the arrogance of man and his presumption of God.

People I meet always seem surprised that I do not hesitate to travel by train, car, airplane or ship when necessary. It is almost as if they expect me to be permanently quivering in my shoes at the thought of a journey. If I acted like that I would have died of fright many years ago – life has to be lived irrespective of the possible dangers and tragedies lurking round the corner. We can only try to be prepared to face them when they arrive.

When I have been on board a ship and read the framed copy of the regulations governing boat drill, lifebelts and lifeboats, I think of the great price we paid for them in the icy waters of the Atlantic Ocean so many years ago. If only there had been enough lifeboats.

EPILOGUE

Miss Eva Miriam Hart died on 14 February 1996, just two weeks after celebrating her ninety-first birthday. She lived long enough to see her biography published and become very successful. Until very near the end of her life she went to great trouble to autograph copies when asked to do so. One of the great pleasures for her was that following publication of her book she and the publishers were invited to the Houses of Parliament in Westminster by Peter Bottomley, MP.

Eva was always worried that once the wreck of the ship was found that it would eventually lead to artifacts being dragged up from the sea-bed and sold. The suggestion that there were great archaeological and historical facts to be determined from the remains never sounded convincing to her and she believed that in most cases the motive was purely a commercial one. She never changed her view that the site of the wreck of the *Titanic* should be respected like any other graveyard.

When the *Titanic* exhibition took place at the National Maritime Museum in Greenwich, London from October 1994 to October 1995 Eva Hart could not bring herself to face going round the exhibition, which contained many items recovered after the wreck had been found. She was always worried that amongst the objects on display there might be things that she would recognise either associated with her family or which she remembered from the ship. However, Eva did attend the dedication of the *Titanic* Memorial Garden at the Museum on 15 April 1995, where she was photographed with another survivor, Edith Brown Haisman. The plaque on the carved stone in the middle of the Memorial Garden reads:

> To
> Commemorate the Sinking
> of
> RMS *Titanic*
> on 15th April 1912
> And All Those Who
> Were Lost With Her
> 15th April 1995

The exhibition was very successful and showed the apparently endless fascination that the tragedy of the ship still has for people. But Eva Hart would have been horrified by the reception given to the film *Titanic* released shortly after her death because of the way in which various actions and people on the ship were misrepresented and the impression that has been gained that what is a work of fiction accurately portrays the events that occurred.

It was a great loss to her many friends when Eva Hart died and many people were amazed by the extent of the obituaries in the British national newspapers to be followed by a totally packed St Chad's Parish Church for the memorial service on Thursday 14 March 1996. The programme for the service intrigued those who attended as it included the statement 'Family, Friends and Visitors are most welcome for Light Refreshments, and "Frogs", in the Church Hall after the Service'.

During her lifetime Eva Hart had collected models and pictures of frogs from all around the world. Friends gave them to her as birthday and Christmas presents or when they returned from vacation. Over the years she acquired hundreds of frogs of all descriptions. There were silver frogs, metal frogs, porcelain frogs, mechanical frogs, frog soap dishes, big frogs, little frogs and cloth frogs. She occasionally asked me what I would do with all her frogs when she died. The frogs were all set out on large tables in the Church Hall after the memorial service and everyone attending took one frog in memory of Eva Miriam Hart. Many of the frogs went back to the people who had given them as presents to Eva over the years.

Shortly after the service we obtained the agreement of the London Borough of Barking and Dagenham to erect a memorial tree in St Chad's recreation ground in Chadwell Heath, where Eva had spent many happy hours walking her dog. Her ashes from cremation were placed at the roots of the tree and a special plaque made and positioned at the foot of the tree as a reminder to the people who pass through the park.

It was a great surprise about a year after her death when Eva's relatives were approached about the possibility of naming a public house after her. The company, Wetherspoons, had purchased the old Police Station in Chadwell Heath and wanted to call it *The Eva Hart* and to have a *Titanic* theme to the decor. Eva would have enjoyed the irony of the suggestion as the Chadwell Heath Police Station was one she knew well from the times that she went there to sign various documents in her role as a magistrate. Agreement was given to the idea and 'Eva Hart' continues to look over the High Street in Chadwell Heath where she lived for so long after returning from the trauma of that sea voyage.

In his book *Night to Remember,* the author Walter Lord wrote of the *Titanic* survivors:

> They all seem to have two qualities in common. First they look marvellous. It is almost as though, having come through this supreme ordeal, they easily surmounted everything else and are now growing old with calm tranquil grace, second, they are wonderfully thoughtful. It seems as if, having witnessed man at his most generous, they scorn any trace of selfishness themselves.

This certainly applied to Eva Hart throughout her life and those of us that knew her remember many kindnesses from her and miss her greatly. Eva Hart was a special person whom it was a privilege to have known, she overcame many setbacks, of which the *Titanic* was only one, and led a full and active life guided by a generosity of spirit.

Ronald C. Denney
Sevenoaks
January 2000

APPENDIX I

Titanic Survivor Archibald Gracie's Account of Lifeboat 14: From His Book, The Truth About the Titanic

Archibald Gracie's memoir of the *Titanic* disaster is probably the most important single source about events of the sinking. Below is reproduced his section on lifeboat 14, the lifeboat Eva and her mother initially escaped on. Gracie researched the story thoroughly and included testimony delivered at the American and British inquiries into the sinking. The testimony below gives further detail of Eva's experiences.

No male passengers in this boat.
Passengers: Mrs Compton, Miss Compton, Mrs Minahan, Miss Minahan, Mrs Collyer, Miss Collyer.
Picked up out of sea: W.F. Hoyt (who died), Steward J. Stewart, and a plucky Japanese.
Women: 50.
Volunteer when crew was short: C. Williams.
Crew: Fifth Officer Lowe, Seaman Scarrot, 2 firemen, Stewards Crowe and Morris.
Stowaway: 1 Italian.
Bade good-bye and sank with ship: Dr Minahan, Mr Compton, Mr Collyer.
Total: 60.

INCIDENTS

H.G. Lowe, Fifth Officer of Titanic (American Titanic Inquiry)

Nos 12, 14 and 16 were down about the same time. I told Mr Moody that three boats had gone away and that an officer ought to go with them. He said: 'You go.' There was difficulty in lowering when I got near the water. I dropped her about five feet, because I was not going to take the chance of being dropped down upon by somebody. While I was on the Boat Deck, two men tried to jump into the boat. I chased them out.

We filled boats 14 and 16 with women and children. Moody filled No. 16 and I filled No. 14. Lightoller was there part of the time. They were all women and children, barring one passenger, who was an Italian, and he sneaked in dressed like a woman. He had a shawl over his head. There was another passenger, a chap by the name of C. Williams, whom I took for rowing. He gave me his name and address (referring to book), 'C. Williams, Racket Champion of the World, 2 Drury Road, Harrow-on-the-Hill, Middlesex, England.'

As I was being lowered, I expected every moment that my boat would be doubled up under my feet. I had overcrowded her, but I knew that I had to take a certain amount of risk. I thought if one additional body was to fall into that boat, that slight additional weight might part the hooks, or carry away something; so as we were coming down past the open decks, I saw a lot of Latin people all along the ship's rails. They were glaring more or less like wild beasts, ready to spring. That is why I yelled out to 'look out,' and let go, bang! right along the ship's side. There was a space I should say of about three feet between the side of the boat and the ship's side, and as I went down I fired these shots without any intention of hurting anybody and with the positive knowledge that I did not hurt anybody. I fired, I think, three times.

Later, 150 yards away, I herded five boats together. I was in No. 14; then I had 10, 12, collapsible 'D' and one other boat (No. 4), and made them tie up. I waited until the yells and shrieks had subsided for the people to thin out, and then I deemed it safe for me to go amongst the wreckage; so I transferred all my passengers, somewhere about fifty-three, from my boat and equally distributed them among my other four boats. Then I asked for volunteers to go with me to the wreck, and it was at this time that I found the Italian. He came aft and had a shawl over his head, and I suppose he had skirts. Anyhow, I pulled the shawl off his face and saw he was a man. He was in a great hurry to get into the other boat and I got hold of him and pitched him in.

Senator Smith: Pitched him in?

Mr Lowe: Yes; because he was not worth being handled better.

Senator Smith: You pitched him in among the women?

Mr Lowe: No, sir; in the forepart of the lifeboat in which I transferred my passengers.

Senator Smith: Did you use some pretty emphatic language when you did this?

Mr Lowe: No, sir; I did not say a word to him. Then I went off and rowed to the wreckage and around the wreckage and picked up four people alive. I do not know who these live persons were. They never came near me afterwards either to say this or that or the other. But one died, Mr W.F. Hoyt, of New York. After we got him in the boat we took his collar off so as to give him more chance to breathe, but unfortunately, he died. He was too far gone when we picked him up. I then left the wreck. I went right around, and, strange to say, I did not see a single female body around the wreckage. I did not have a light in my boat. Then I could see the *Carpathia* coming up and I thought: 'Well, I am the fastest boat of the lot,' as I was sailing, you see. I was going through the water four or five knots, bowling along very nicely.

By and by, I noticed a collapsible boat, Engelhardt 'D.' It looked rather sorry, so I thought: 'Well, I will go down and pick her up and make sure of her. This was Quartermaster Bright's boat. Mrs H.B. Harris, of New York, was in it. She had a broken arm. I had taken this first collapsible ('D') in tow and I noticed that there was another collapsible ('A') in a worse plight than this one that I had in tow. I got to her just in time and took off, I suppose, about twenty men and one lady. I left three male bodies in it. I may have been a bit hard-hearted in doing this. I thought: 'I am not here to worry about bodies; I am here to save life and not bother about bodies.' The people on the raft told me these had been dead for some time. I do not know whether any one endeavored to find anything on their persons that would identify them, because they were all up to their ankles in water when I took them off.

Joseph Scarrot, A.B. (British Titanic Inquiry)

I myself took charge of No. 14 as the only sailorman there. The Chief Officer ordered women and children to be taken in. Some men came and tried to rush the boat. They were foreigners and could not understand the orders I gave them, but I managed to keep them away. I had to use some persuasion with a boat tiller. One man jumped in twice and I had to throw him out the third time. I got all the women and children into the boat. There were fifty-four women and four children – one of them a baby in arms. There were myself, two firemen, three or four stewards and Mr Lowe, who got into the boat. I told him the trouble I had with the men and he brought out his revolver and fired two shots and said: 'If there is any more trouble I will fire at them.' The shots fired were fired between the boat and the ship's side. The after fall got twisted and we dropped the boat by the releasing gear and got clear of the ship. There were four men rowing. There was a man in the boat who we thought was a sailor, but he was not. He was a window cleaner. The *Titanic* was then about fifty yards off and we lay there with the other boats. Mr Lowe was at the helm. We went in the direction of the cries and came among hundreds of dead bodies and life belts. We got one man, who died shortly after he got into the boat. One of the stewards tried to restore him, but without avail. There was another man who was calling for help, but among the bodies and wreckage it was too late for us to reach him. It took half an hour to get to that man. Cannot say exactly, but think we got about twenty off of the Engelhardt boat ('A').

E.J. Buley, A.B. (American Titanic Inquiry)
(After his transfer from No. 10 to No. 14.) Then, with Lowe in his boat No. 14, I went back to where the *Titanic* sank and picked up the remaining live bodies. We got four; all the others were dead. We turned over several to see if they were alive. It looked as if none of them were drowned. They looked as if frozen. The life belts they had on were that much (indicating) out of the water, and their heads lay back with their faces on the water. They were head and shoulders out of water, with their heads thrown back. In the morning, after we had picked up all that were alive, there was a collapsible boat ('A') swamped, which we saw with a lot of people up to their knees in water. We sailed over to them. We then picked up another boat ('D') and took her in tow. I think we were about the seventh or eighth boat alongside the *Carpathia*.

F.O. Evans, A.B. (American Titanic Inquiry)
So from No. 10 we got into his (Lowe's) boat, No. 14, and went straight over towards the wreckage with eight or nine men and picked up four persons alive, one of whom died on the way to the *Carpathia*. Another picked up was named J. Stewart, a steward. You could not hardly count the number of dead bodies. I was afraid to look over the sides because it might break my nerves down. We saw no other

people in the water or heard their cries, other than these four picked up. The officer said: 'Hoist a sail forward.' I did so and made sail in the direction of the collapsible boat 'A' about a mile and a half away, which had been swamped. There were in it one woman and about ten or eleven men. Then we picked up another collapsible boat ('D') and took her in tow to the *Carpathia*. There were then about twenty-five people in our boat No. 14, including the one who died.

One of the ladies there passed over a flask of whisky to the people who were all wet through. She asked if anybody needed the spirits, and these people were all soaking wet and nearly perished and they passed it around among these men and women. It took about twenty minutes after we sighted the *Carpathia* to get alongside of her. We saw five or six icebergs – some of them tremendous, about the height of the *Titanic* – and field ice. After we got on the *Carpathia* we saw, at a rough estimate, a twenty-five mile floe, sir, flat like the floor.

F. Crowe, steward (American Titanic Inquiry)

I assisted in handing the women and children into boat No. 12, and was asked if I could take an oar. I said: 'Yes,' and was told to man the boat, I believe, by Mr Murdoch. After getting the women and children in we lowered down to within four or five feet of the water, and then the block and tackle got twisted in some way, causing us to have to cut the ropes to allow the boat to get into the water. This officer, Lowe, told us to do this. He was in the boat with us. I stood by the lever – the lever releasing the blocks from the hooks in the boat. He told me to wait, to get away and cut the line to raise the lever, thereby causing the hooks to open and allow the boat to drop in the water.

There was some shooting that occurred at the time the boat was lowered. There were various men passengers, probably Italians or some foreign nationality other than English or American, who attempted to 'rush' the boats. The officers threatened to shoot any man who put his foot into the boat. An officer fired a revolver, but either downward or upward, not shooting at any one of the passengers at all and not injuring anybody. He fired perfectly clear upward and downward and stopped the rush. There was no disorder after that. One woman cried, but that was all. There was no panic or anything in the boat.

After getting into the water I pushed out to the other boats. In No. 14 there were fifty-seven women and children and about six men, including one officer, and I may have been seven. I am not quite sure. I know how many, because when we got out a distance the officer asked me how many people were in the boat. When the boat was released and fell I think she must have sprung a leak. A lady stated that there was some water coming up over her ankles. Two men and this lady assisted in bailing it out I with bails that were kept in the boat for that purpose. We transferred our people to other boats so as to return to the wreck and see if we could pick up anybody else. Returning to the wreck we heard various cries and endeavored to get among them, and we were successful in doing so, and picked up one body that was floating around in the water. It was that of a man, and he expired shortly afterwards. Going further into the wreckage we came across a steward (J. Stewart) and got him into the boat. He was very cold and his hands were kind of stiff. He recovered by the time that we got back to the *Carpathia.*

A Japanese or Chinese young fellow that we picked up on top of some wreckage, which may have been a sideboard or a table that was floating around, also survived. We stopped (in the wreckage) until daybreak, and we saw in the distance an Engelhardt collapsible boat ('A') with a crew of men in it. We went over to the boat, and found twenty men and one woman; also three dead bodies, which we left. Returning under sail we took another collapsible boat in tow (boat 'D') containing fully sixty people, women and children. I did not see the iceberg that struck the ship. When it came daylight and we could see, there were two or three bergs around, and one man pointed out that that must have been the berg, and another man pointed out another berg. Really, I do not think anybody knew which one struck the ship.

Mrs Charlotte Collyer, third class passenger, in The Semi-Monthly Magazine, May, 1912
A little further on we saw a floating door that must have been torn loose when the ship went down. Lying upon it, face downward, was a small Japanese. He had lashed himself with a rope to his frail raft, using the broken hinges to make the knots secure. As far as we could see, he was dead. The sea washed over him every time the door bobbed up and down, and he was frozen stiff. He did not answer when he was hailed, and the officer hesitated about trying to save him.

'What's the use?' said Mr Lowe. 'He's dead, likely, and if he isn't there's others better worth saving than a Jap!'

He had actually turned our boat around, but he changed his mind and went back. The Japanese was hauled on board, and one of the women rubbed his chest, while others chafed his hands and feet.

In less time than it takes to tell, he opened his eyes. He spoke to us in his own tongue; then, seeing that we did not understand, he struggled to his feet, stretched his arms above his head, stamped his feet and in five minutes or so had almost recovered his strength. One of the sailors near to him was so tired that he could hardly pull his oar. The Japanese bustled over, pushed him from his seat, took his oar and worked like a hero until we were finally picked up. I saw Mr Lowe watching him in open-mouthed surprise.

'By Jove!' muttered the officer, 'I'm ashamed of what I said about the little blighter. I'd save the likes o' him six times over if I got the chance.'

Miss Minahan's affidavit (American Titanic Inquiry)
After the *Titanic* went down the cries were horrible. Some of the women implored Officer Lowe of No. 10 to divide his passengers among the three other boats and go back to rescue them. His first answer to these requests was: 'You ought to be damn glad you are here and have got your own life.' After some time he was persuaded to do as he was asked. As I came up to him to be transferred to the other boat he said 'Jump, God damn you, jump.' I had shown no hesitancy and was waiting until my turn. He had been so blasphemous during the hours we were in his boat that the women in my end of the boat all thought he was under the influence of liquor. (Testimony elsewhere shows that Officer Lowe is a teetotaler.) Then he took all the men who had rowed No. 14, together with the men from other boats, and went back to the scene of the wreck. We were left with a steward and a stoker to row our boat, which was crowded. The steward did his best, but the stoker refused at first to row, but finally helped two men who were the only ones pulling on that side. It was just four o'clock when we sighted the *Carpathia*, and we were three hours getting to her. On the *Carpathia* we were treated with every kindness and given every comfort possible.

The above affidavit being of record shows Officer Lowe in an unfortunate, bad light. There is no doubt of it that he was intemperate in his language only. In all other respects he was a first-class officer, as proven by what he accomplished. But I am glad that I have the account of another lady passenger in the same boat which is a tribute to what he did. I met Officer Lowe in Washington the time that both of us were summoned before the U.S. Court of Inquiry, and I am quite sure that the only point against him is that he was a little hasty in speech in the accomplishment of his work.

Miss Compton, who lost her brother, I had the pleasure of meeting on the *Carpathia*. She is still a sufferer from injuries received in the wreck, and yet has been very kind in sending me an account of her experience, from which I cite the following:

> As she stood on the rail to step into boat No. 14 it was impossible to see whether she would step into the boat or into the water. She was pushed into the boat with such violence that she found herself on her hands and knees, but fortunately landed on a coil of rope.

This seemed to be the general experience of the women. All the passengers entered the lifeboat at the same point and were told to move along to make place for those who followed. This was difficult, as the thwarts were so high that it was difficult to climb over them, encumbered as the ladies were with lifebelts. It was a case of throwing one's self over rather than climbing over.

Miss Compton from her place in the stern of the lifeboat overheard the conversation between Officer Lowe and another officer, which the former gave in his testimony.

Just before the boat was lowered a man jumped in. He was immediately hauled out. Mr Lowe then pulled his revolver and said: 'If anyone else tries that this is what he will get.' He then fired his revolver in the air.

She mentions the same difficulties, elsewhere recorded, about the difficulties in lowering the boat, first the stern very high, and then the bow; also how the ropes were cut and No. 14 struck the water hard. At this time the count showed 58 in the boat, and a later one made the number 60. A child near her answered in neither of the counts.

'Mr Lowe's manly bearing,' she says, 'gave us all confidence. As I look back now he seems to me to personify the best traditions of the British sailor. He asked us all to try and find a lantern, but none was to be found. Mr Lowe had with him, however, an electric light which he flashed from time to time. Almost at once the boat began to leak and in a few moments the women in the forward part of the boat were standing in water. There was nothing to bail with and I believe the men used their hats.'

'Officer Lowe insisted on having the mast put up. He crawled forward and in a few moments the mast was raised and ready. He said this was necessary as no doubt with dawn there would be a breeze. He returned to his place and asked the stewards and firemen, who were acting as crew, if they had any matches, and insisted on having them passed to him. He then asked if they had any tobacco and said: "Keep it in your pockets, for tobacco makes you thirsty." Mr Lowe wished to remain near the ship that he might have a chance to help someone after she sank. Some of the women protested and he replied: "I don't like to leave her, but if you feel that way about it we will pull away a little distance.'"

Miss Compton's account corroborates other information about boat No. 14, which we have elsewhere. She was among the number transferred to Engelhardt boat 'D.' 'I now found myself,' she said, 'in the stern of a collapsible boat. In spite of Mr Lowe's warning the four small boats began to separate, each going its own way. Soon it seemed as though our boat was the only one on the sea. We went through a great deal of wreckage. The men who were supposed to be rowing – one was a fireman – made no effort to keep away from it. They were all the time looking towards the horizon. With daylight we saw the *Carpathia*, and not so very long afterwards Officer Lowe, sailing towards us, for, as he had predicted, quite a strong breeze had sprung up. We caught the rope which he threw us from the stern of his boat. Someone in ours succeeded in catching it and we were taken in tow to the *Carpathia*.'

APPENDIX 2

The White Star Liners – Olympic, Titanic and Britannic [This was actually the second ship that the White Star Line named Britannic. The name had previously been given to a much smaller liner many years earlier and was re-used following the sinking of the Titanic.]

The only technical details about the *Titanic* included in the foregoing pages are those which are essential to the biography itself. However, the following information is included for the benefit of those readers who are interested in the three sister ships and their histories.

At the time of the *Titanic* disaster the White Star Line was owned by the International Mercantile Marine Company of the USA. The three liners were all built at Harland and Wolff's dockyard in Belfast and were intended to be the most luxurious ocean going liners afloat, in order to capture the lucrative transatlantic traffic.

The *Olympic* was the first to be commissioned and made her maiden voyage on 14 June 1911. She and the *Titanic* were almost identical in size, being 882.5 feet long and 92.5 feet wide at the widest point. The *Titanic* was the heavier of the two by 1,004 tonnes, with a gross tonnage of 46,328. The third sister, the *Britannic,* was made wider at 94 feet and her gross tonnage was 48,158, the extra weight being brought about by the incorporation of safety features made necessary as a result of the *Titanic* disaster.

The *Olympic* was also modified structurally following the sinking of the *Titanic* and shortly after was used as a troop ship throughout the First World War, during which she managed to sink a German U-boat by ramming it. She survived the war and later returned to work as a passenger liner, continuing in use until 1935 after which she was scrapped. Of the three ships she was the only one to lead a full life of service.

The *Titanic* was intended to be even more luxurious than the *Olympic* and designed to carry more passengers. She was launched on 31 May 1911 and commenced her fateful maiden voyage on Wednesday 10 April 1912. First class accommodation included a gymnasium, a miniature golf course, a squash court and a swimming pool. Even the third class (steerage) facilities were considered to be exceptional for ships of that era.

Her reputation for being unsinkable arose from the design features that gave her considerable strength and rigidity. It was considered that the cellular double bottom and the fifteen transverse bulkheads would be more than sufficient to cope with any impact at sea. The only incident she was not proof against was an impact below the waterline sufficient to tear open more than four of the watertight compartments. For, although the *Titanic* possessed a double bottom, she had not been given a double shell up the sides to above the water-line. This omission was much commented upon after the tragedy as the *Great Eastern* had shown the value of a double shell – a feature incorporated in 1858 – more than half a century earlier.

It was originally intended that the *Britannic* should be called the *Gigantic,* but it was felt that this was tempting fate and the name was changed, while the ship was still under construction, after the *Titanic* was lost. She never saw service as a passenger liner, being immediately pressed into service as a hospital ship when commissioned in December 1915. Eleven months later, on 21 November 1916, she was sunk in the Aegean while making her seventh trip to pick up wounded soldiers at Gallipoli. Twenty-one people lost their lives and for many years it was uncertain whether the ship was sunk by a torpedo or by a sea-mine. In 1977, Commander Jacques Cousteau, the underwater explorer, was reported to have found evidence that the cause of the sinking was a hole made by a torpedo, but it was felt that it may also have struck or detonated a mine after the initial explosion had taken place.

It is difficult to imagine the impact that the three luxury liners would have made on the Atlantic run if they had been in service simultaneously. They could easily have monopolised the North American traffic for many years but for the *Titanic* disaster.

BIBLIOGRAPHY

Books and Periodicals

Anderson, Roy (1964) *White Star,* Prescot, England: T Stephenson and Sons Ltd.

Ballard, Dr Robert D. (1987) *The Discovery of the Titanic*, Toronto: Madison Press; London: Hodder & Stoughton.

Baton, John P. and Haas, Charles A. (1987) *Titanic, Destination Disaster,* New York: W. W. Norton & Co.

Beesley, Lawrence (1912) *The Loss of the 'Titanic',* London: Phillip Allan & Co. Ltd, reprinted in the Nautilus Library, 1929.

Behe, George (1988) *Titanic, Psychic Forewarnings of a Tragedy,* Wellingborough, UK: The Aquarian Press.

Biel, Stephen (1996) *Down with the Old Canoe,* New York & London: W. W. Norton & Co.

Booth, John and Coughlan, Scan (1993) *Titanic – Signals of Disaster,* Westbury, UK: White Star Publications.

Committee on Commerce (1912) *Titanic Disaster,* Report of the Committee on Commerce, United States Senate, Washington DC (1912). Republished by 7C's Press Inc., Riverside, CT (1975).

Dodge, Washington (1912) *The Loss of the Titanic*, an address given to the Commonwealth Club, San Francisco, 11 May 1912.

Gardiner, Robin and Van der Vat, Dan (1995) *The Riddle of the Titanic*, London: Weidenfeld and Nicolson.

Geller, Judith (1998) *Titanic. Women and Children First,* Sparkford, UK: Patrick Stephens.

Gibbs, Sir Phillip (1912) *The Deathless Story of the Titanic*, London: Lloyds Weekly News.

Gracie, Colonel Archibald (1913) *The Truth about the Titanic*, Connecticut; reprinted 7C's Press Inc., 1973.

Harrison, Leslie (1992) *A Titanic Myth,* Worcester, UK: The S.PA. Ltd., Hanicy Swan, 2nd revised ed.

Hyslop, Donald, Forsyth, Alastair and Jemima, Sheila (1994) *Titanic Voices,* Southampton, UK: Southampton City Council, Oral History.

Lord, Walter (1956) *A Night to Remember,* London: Longmans, Green & Co. Ltd.

Lord, Walter (1986) *The Night Lives On,* New York: Viking Penguin.

Lynch, Don (1992) *Titanic: An Illustrated History,* London: Hodder & Stoughton; Toronto: Madison Press.

McCluskie, Tom, Sharpe, Michael and Marriott, Leo (1998) *Titanic and her Sisters Olympic and Britannic,* London: Parkgate Books.

Marcus, Geoffrey (1960) *The Maiden Voyage,* New York: Viking Press, Inc.

Reade, Leslie edited by Edward P. De Groot (1993) *The Ship That Stood Still,* Yeovil, UK: Patrick Stephen Ltd.

Robertson, Morgan (1898) *The Wreck of the Titan or Futility,* Connecticut: republished by 7C's Press Inc., 1974.

Rostron, Sir Arthur H. (1931) *Home from the Sea,* London: Cassell & Co.

Scientific American (1912) Articles in issues of 27th April, 11th May, 18th May and 8th June.

They Called Her Unsinkable, in *Disaster* (1975) London: Phoebus Publishing Co. and BPC Publishing Ltd.

Titanic Historical Society, *Titanic Commutator,* periodically published by the *Titanic* Historical Society, PO Box 53, Indian Orchard, Massachusetts, USA.

Wincour, Jack (ed) (1960) *The Story of the Titanic as Told by its Survivors,* New York: Dover Publications Inc.

Records

1. *Titanic,* LBP 1050, Vantage Recording Co. (1973)
2. *The Sinking of the Titanic,* by Gavin Bryars, Obscure, Island Records Ltd, (1975)

Internet

BBC interview with Eva Hart 1987, listen to it by going to www.bbc.co.uk/archive/titanic/5058.shtml

THE AUTHOR

Dr Ronald C. Denney is a well known author and broadcaster, having written articles for the *Sunday Telegraph* and the *New Scientist* amongst many others.

He is the author and co-author of more than twenty books on technical and environmental subjects, including one on pollution and four on drinking and driving, and has written a children's story. This is his first biographical subject. He is married, has two children and lives in Kent. His main occupation is as an independent Forensic Scientist and Industrial Consultant.

Dr Denney and Miss Hart were friends for many years and, as the author of the biography, he was given access to Miss Hart's private papers including personal communications concerned with the *Titanic* disaster and its aftermath. He acted as one of her executors after her death in 1996.

LIST OF ILLUSTRATIONS

Also available from Amberley Publishing

The story of the sinking of the Titanic *based on first-hand accounts collected in the days and weeks following the disaster*

'If you only read one book about *Titanic*, read this one; if you've read every book published about the *Titanic*, read this one again' NAUTILUS INTENATIONAL TELEGRAPH

On Thursday 22 May 1912, a mere 37 days after the sinking, respected London publisher Grant Richards, delivered Filson Young's book to booksellers around the capital. Both Filson and Grant knew victims of the sinking and both worked hard to gather first-hand testimony to use in the book. Much of his telling of the story still stands today and his speculations about the feeling of daily life aboard the doomed ship are used in books and films on the subject.

£16.99 Hardback
92 illustrations
160 pages
978-1-4456-0407-7

Available from all good bookshops or to order direct
Please call **01453-847-800**
www.amberleybooks.com

Also Available from Amberley Publishing

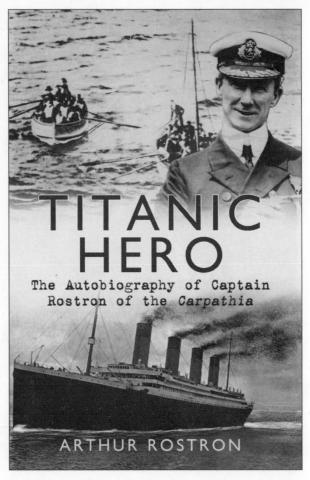

The story of the Titanic in the words of the hero who's swift action save the lives of over 700 survivors

£16.99 Paperback
39 illustrations
192 pages
978-1-4456-0420-6

Available from all good bookshops or to order direct
Please call **01453–847–800**
www.amberleybooks.com

Also available from Amberley Publishing

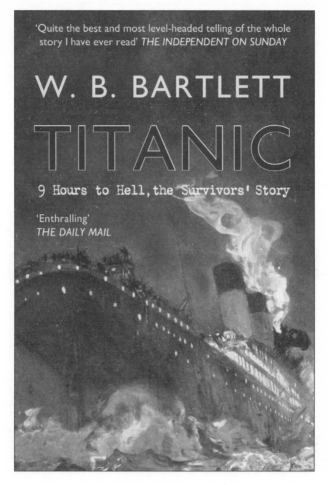

A major new history of the disaster that weaves into the narrative the first-hand accounts of those who survived

'Enthralling' THE DAILY MAIL
'Quite the best and most level-headed telling of the whole story I have ever read'
THE INDEPENDENT ON SUNDAY

It was twenty minutes to midnight on Sunday 14 April, when Jack Thayer felt the Titanic lurch to port, a motion followed by the slightest of shocks. Seven-year old Eva Hart barely noticed anything was wrong. For Stoker Fred Barrett, shovelling coal down below, it was somewhat different; the side of the ship where he was working caved in. For the next nine hours, Jack, Eva and Fred faced death and survived. 1600 people did not. This is the story told through the eyes of Jack, Eva, Fred and over a hundred others of those who survived and recorded their experiences.

£9.99 Paperback
72 illustrations (14 colour)
368 pages
978-1-4456-0482-4

Available from all good bookshops or to order direct
Please call **01453-847-800**
www.amberleybooks.com

Also available from Amberley Publishing

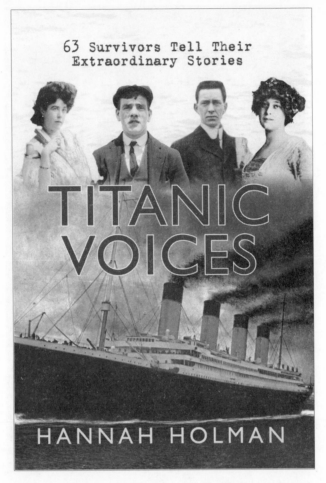

The sinking of the Titanic *in the words of the survivors*

There were 712 survivors of the *Titanic* disaster and their horrific experience has captivated readers and movie goers for almost 100 years. But what was it actually like for a woman to say goodbye to her husband? For a mother to leave her teenage sons? For the unlucky many who found themselves in the freezing Atlantic waters? *Titanic Voices* is the most comprehensive collection of *Titanic* survivors' accounts ever published and includes many unpublished, and long forgotten accounts, unabridged, together with an authoritative editorial commentary. It is also the first book to include substantial accounts from women survivors – most of the previously well known accounts were written by men.

£20 Hardback
135 illustrations (11 colour)
512 pages
978-1-4456-0222-6

Available from all good bookshops or to order direct
Please call **01453-847-800**
www.amberleybooks.com

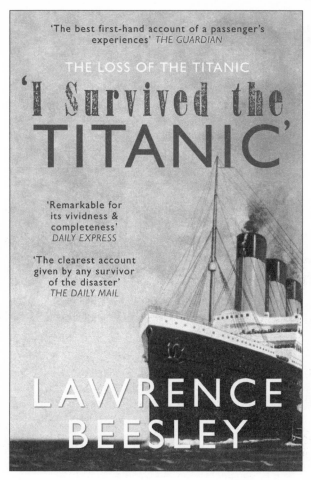

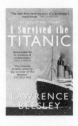